The Child's View of Reading

Related Titles of Interest

Thoughts That Begin Students' Day, K–2
Cathy Collins Block and JoAnn Zinke
ISBN: 0-205-14691-0

126 Strategies to Build Language Arts Abilities: A Month-by-Month Resource
Cathy Collins
ISBN: 0-205-13025-9

Integrating Reading and Writing through Children's Literature
Kathy Everts Danielson and Janice LaBonty
ISBN: 0-205-15314-3

Literacy Development through the Integrated Language Arts
Lesley Mandel Morrow, Louise Cherry Wilkinson, and Jeffrey Smith
ISBN: 0-205-14735-6 Paper   0-205-14736-4 Cloth

Developing Cultural Literacy through the Writing Process
Barbara C. Palmer, Mary L. Hafner, and Marilyn F. Sharp
ISBN: 0-205-13989-2

A Handbook for the K–12 Reading Resource Specialist
Marguerite C. Radencich, Penny G. Beers, and Jeanne Shay Schumm
ISBN: 0-205-14081-5

A Green Dinosaur Day: A Guide for Developing Thematic Units in Literature-Based Instruction, K–6
Patricia L. Roberts
ISBN: 0-205-14007-6

▶

The Child's View of Reading

Understandings for Teachers and Parents

Pamela A. Michel
State University of New York College at Oswego

Line drawings by Michael Ancillotti

Allyn and Bacon
Boston • London • Toronto • Sydney • Tokyo • Singapore

Library of Congress Cataloging-in-Publication Data

Michel, Pamela A.
   The child's view of reading : understandings for teachers and parents / Pamela A. Michel.
      p. cm.
   Includes bibliographical references (p.   ) and index.
   ISBN 0-205-13784-9
   1. Reading.   2. Children—Attitudes.   3. Comprehension in children.   I. Title.
   LB1050.2.M53   1994
   372.41—dc20   93-24104

Printed in the United States of America

10 9 8 7 6 5 4 3 2   97 96 95 94 93

To my grandfather Joseph Glass
and
my daughter Tamara with love.

About the Author

Pamela A. Michel earned her B.A. in Music and Elementary Education from Elmira College in 1975. She received both her M.S. and Ph.D. in Reading Education from Syracuse University. She is currently an Associate Professor of Reading in the Elementary Education Department at the State University of New York College at Oswego. Dr. Michel served as the director of the Syracuse University Reading Clinic and the assistant director of the Syracuse University Reading Program for Developmentally Disabled Adults prior to completing her doctoral studies in 1988. As a former elementary school teacher and reading specialist for twelve years, she has a special interest in early literacy acquisition, qualitative research methodology, and assessment and instruction of students with reading disabilities. She resides in Baldwinsville, New York, with her husband, Dan, and daughter, Tamara.

Contents

Preface   xiii

Acknowledgments   xv

1 Introduction   **1**
Preview   2
Amy Anderson (Age 6)   2
A First-Grade Teacher Remembers   4
Early Research   5
Recent Studies   8
The Child's Perspective   11
A Classroom Teacher Responds...   12
Parents Respond...   30

2 The Study: Listening Questions   **17**
Preview   18
The Classroom   18
Data Collection   20
Listening Questions   23
Teacher as Researcher   28
A Classroom Teacher Responds...   29
Parents Respond...   30

3 Tasks: Circling, Underlining, and Crossing Out   33

Preview   34
First-Grade Reading Groups: What Goes On   34
Children's Perceptions: Tasks   35
Home-School Dichotomy   43
A Classroom Teacher Responds…   48
Parents Respond…   49

4 Processing Print: More Than Just Sounds   51

Preview   52
Mr. Frank's Reading Group   52
Children's Perceptions: Process   53
Process: How It Comes to Be   57
A Classroom Teacher Responds…   61
Parents Respond…   62

5 Purpose: Whose?   65

Preview   66
The Babysitter   66
Children's Perceptions: Reasons for Reading   68
A Classroom Teacher Responds…   73
Parents Respond…   74

6 Reading Groups: Hard Cover/Soft Cover   77

Preview   78
Sarah's in a Hard-Cover Book   78
Children's Perceptions: How Am I Doing?   80
Feelings Change over Time   83
A Classroom Teacher Responds…   89
Parents Respond…   90

7 Standardized Test Time: Get a Good Night's Sleep   93

Preview   94
Two Teachers' Views   94
Children's Perceptions: Standardized Test Time   95
Parents' Role   99
A Classroom Teacher Responds…   106
Parents Respond…   107

8 Home: The Beginning   109

Preview   110
Doing Homework   110
Home: Where Children Learn to Read   111
Homework: Parent-Child Conflict   112
Parents: The Natural Role   117
A Classroom Teacher Responds...   119
Parents Respond...   120

9 Siblings: Teachers and Learners   123

Preview   124
Melissa Teaches Fred to Read   124
Older Siblings as Teachers   124
A Classroom Teacher Responds...   132
Parents Respond...   133

10 Reading: Through the Child's Eyes   135

Preview   136
Listen to Children   136
Children Have Rich Perceptions   139
Gauging Instructional Effectiveness   142
A Classroom Teacher Responds...   143
Parents Respond...   145

References   147

Works Mentioned   151

Index   153

Preface

"I'm learnin' to read." Many a proud first-grader has reported this fact to family and friends. We hear the words, we think we understand, but few of us recognize the enormous significance of the words to the speaker—the young reader—and seldom do we probe to find out exactly what the emerging reader means as she utters the sentence. We hear, but we may not *listen* as well as we might to find the hidden treasure within the mind and spirit of the child who is on the verge of entering into the world of literacy.

This book is about young children and how they think about reading. It is written from the point of view of the child and therefore can be termed *child-centered* or perhaps even *child-driven*.

A premise of this book is that beginning readers have rich understandings of reading and are able to share these insights with any adults who care to listen. The book argues that reading instruction can be improved by listening to children and adjusting instruction accordingly.

The ideas developed in this book are data-driven. That is, they are grounded in extensive research conducted with beginning readers, their teachers, parents, and siblings. The findings of this text challenge those who argue that young children are often confused and mistaken about reading. Contained in each chapter are revealing "snapshots" of real classroom environments. Classroom anecdotes and children's quotations bring the research to life and demonstrate to even the most skeptical reader that young children do indeed have rich and insightful understandings of the world of beginning reading that they experience on a day-to-day basis.

This book does not advocate any single method of reading instruction other than simply listening to children and responding to what they say about their reading. It would be inappropriate, if not impossible, to provide readers of this text with a list of instructional do's and don't's or a set of curricular guidelines to follow with all children. To do so would be a contradiction, as this text challenges teachers to listen to children and use their perceptions as a gauge of instructional effectiveness. One might say that first-graders get both the first and last word on all issues presented, as the research was designed from the onset to present reading from their perspective. This book does not present reading from the teacher's point of view. If this book were written about teachers, *their* stories and the complexities of their work would have been told, making the text much more sympathetic to their position.

This book celebrates children and validates their views of learning to read. Sadly, it does not always celebrate teaching, as the book documents how beginning reading instruction is often counterproductive to learning to read. Through children's words you will discover that many first-graders who enter school as confident, eager "readers," end their first-grade experience with little confidence in themselves, not only as readers but as learners.

The book is based on my teaching experience and my research into children's perceptions of reading. It is a distillation of hundreds of hours of observations and interviews with parents, teachers, and young children. The events depicted in this book were either directly observed by me in their natural setting or reported to me during interviews. Standard qualitative research methods were utilized in data gathering and analysis. And, in the tradition of qualitative research reporting, this book was written from the perspective of those studied as opposed to that of those doing the studying. Throughout the book, readers are encouraged in the qualitative tradition to "listen to children" and, in doing so, to become practitioners of qualitative inquiry.

An anecdotal account taken from my field notes introduces each chapter. Each chapter also contains a section called "A Classroom Teacher Responds...," which contains a written response from Barbara Parry, an elementary school teacher with eighteen years of teaching experience. Barbara is a highly competent teacher who welcomes new ideas, has a unique understanding of children, and was willing to share her knowledge and experiences with others. Her responses are insightful and identify important instructional implications.

In addition, each chapter contains a section called "Parents Respond..." from Susan and Bob Underwood. The Underwoods are parents of two girls, ages 8 and 11, and a 6-year-old boy. They have lived through their fair share of reading stories, first days of school, hard-covered readers, and standardized tests. They have paid their dues and, as parents, bring an important and frequently neglected perspective to the schooling issues discussed in this book.

Some refer to the practices advocated in this book as "kidwatching," while others may cast these practices in terms of "teacher as researcher." I prefer simply to speak in terms of "listening to children." What matters is not the label, but rather acknowledging the young child as a thinking, knowing, understanding being, perfectly capable of enlightening adults as to what is really happening when a child says, "I'm learnin' to read."

Acknowledgments

For their personal and professional support toward the completion of this book, my sincerest gratitude is extended to the following individuals:

I thank the members of my dissertation committee: Professors Diane J. Sawyer, Robert Bogdan, and Margaret Lay-Dopyera for the help that each gave at various stages of my research, which is the foundation of this book. Diane has been a mentor and friend for the last fifteen years. Her scholarship, uncompromising integrity, commitment to excellence, and dedication to her work has shaped my professional life. Robert Bogdan provided a theoretical framework for my study and taught me the craft of qualitative research. His research perspective and insights have been an inspiration to me, and have greatly influenced my thinking. Margaret Lay-Dopyera's sensitivity and understanding of young children had a profound effect on this study. I am also grateful to Professor Peter Mosenthal for the support and intellectual stimulation he offered me throughout my graduate studies.

Claudia Gentile, my "soul-mate" at Syracuse, was a sounding board for my ideas as I formulated this study. Our friendship and daily professional sharing enriched both my life and my work.

My colleagues and friends at SUNY Oswego have been very supportive and encouraging throughout the preparation of this manuscript. I would like to thank three in particular who personify academic colleagueship.

Claire Putala's critical thinking and scholarship have been a constant source of intellectual stimulation to me. I have profited immeasurably from her ideas, comments, and friendship. Her good work and constant support are greatly appreciated.

I thank Cindy Ewers for her friendship and for casting a critical eye over the pages of this manuscript on more than a few occasions. She has provided me with excellent feedback and constructive criticism, which have contributed much to the writing of this book.

Sharon Kane never tired of reading my manuscript and sharpening my writing. She has read and reread every draft of every chapter. Her thoughtful editing, additions to the manuscript, knowledge of the field of reading, and commitment to children have been a source of inspiration and helped shape this book. Sharon is a true friend who has willingly given of herself, and I am forever grateful.

There is no adequate way of acknowledging my friend and colleague Craig Dougherty. He has been involved in this work from the beginning. We have talked about children's perceptions since the day I decided to pursue this area for my dissertation study. His voice can be heard throughout the pages of this book. I am deeply indebted to him for all of his contributions.

Special thanks to former graduate students Trasie Allbright and Denise Yourth, who assisted me in conducting interviews with older siblings. They helped me understand the significant role older siblings play in the reading development of their younger brothers and sisters.

A special note of thanks to Kathy Daunce, who knows how to put a project together, and thereby freed my attention for writing efforts on more than one occasion.

I wish to express my appreciation to Mike Ancillotti, whose sensitive drawings help bring the pages of this book to life.

Barbara Parry is a teacher who cares enough about children to devote hours of her time to respond to each chapter of this book. Her reactions provide readers with important instructional insights. I thank her for her dedication and commitment to teaching.

Susan and Bob Underwood have provided readers of this book with information that is all too often omitted. Their experience and perspective as parents has enriched this text significantly. I thank them for their contribution.

I owe much to my editors at Allyn and Bacon. I thank Mylan Jaixen for his interest and enthusiasm during the early stages of this book, and Susan Hutchinson for guiding me to its completion. Special thanks to Judy Ashkenaz for her thoughtful suggestions and careful editing. I also thank the following reviewers for their insightful comments and suggestions: Margaret Naughton of the Somerville School System in Somerville, Massachusetts; David Hayes of the University of Georgia; Jeanne Schumm of the University of Miami; and Susan Trostle of the University of Rhode Island.

My parents, Dave and Lorraine Forst, and my sisters, Cynde, Debbie, and Lisa, have contributed indirectly to the creation of this book. Each, in unique ways, has supported me and always recognized what I have needed to be. I could make the promise of "lighter" times to come, but they know better. I am grateful for their love and understanding.

A special note of gratitude is due my family, Danny and Tamara. They have provided love, encouragement, understanding, and a willingness to let me strive and grow, even though the price was high. Danny has supported me and my work in all ways, including helping me retype this manuscript over and over. Tamara, my daughter, is a constant reminder of what is truly important in life and personifies the beauty of children.

Most important, this book would not have been possible without the children and the cooperation of their parents and teachers. I could never thank them enough for all they have taught me.

▶ 1

Introduction

PREVIEW

This chapter may expose you to an entirely new way of thinking about children and how they come to understand reading. It may encourage you to view both reading and teaching through the eyes of the child. It may also convince you that young children have valuable insights about reading, although their perceptions may not always match those of adults.

In addition, this chapter will summarize some of the key research conducted in the area of children's perceptions of reading and show how much of the focus has shifted from an adult-driven to a child-driven perspective.

After reading this chapter, you may better understand how to view children's perceptions of reading and how your view can be adjusted to focus more clearly on what and how children think. You may also develop a better understanding of how informal interviews and participant observation contribute to that understanding.

AMY ANDERSON (AGE 6)

I had been observing Amy Anderson and the twenty-eight other children in her first-grade classroom for over a week before I had the chance to speak with her directly. After talking with Amy for several minutes about some work I had observed her doing in class, I asked her the simple question, "What is reading?" Amy paused a second, turned her head, and replied, "I used to think reading was making sense of a story, but now I know it's just letters." I hesitated, trying to conceal the shock and amazement that I was feeling at Amy's remark. I thanked her for talking to me and began pondering the meaning and implications of her comment.

Initially, I thought that Amy must be either confused or mistaken. That is, she couldn't possibly see reading now as "just letters." In the course of my research, I had previously examined her school district's reading goals and objectives and found them to be holistic and comprehension-oriented. The goals included statements such as, "All children will view reading as a meaning-oriented activity," "Children will learn to appreciate literature," and "Children will comprehend what they have read."

The district had also developed a literacy philosophy, as follows:

Literacy is the ability to use language to communicate effectively. Reading, writing, speaking and listening are language processes that complement and support each other. Our goal is to provide an integrated language-rich environment that ensures students will reach their full potential as lifelong learners through literacy.

My initial conversations with Amy's teacher indicated that the teacher ascribed to a "comprehension-oriented" approach to the teaching of reading, and the basal reader she used in class "stressed comprehension." The teacher's manual of the basal reader she was using with Amy clearly stated in many ways that comprehension was critical to this reading program. Amy's teacher remarked:

> *I want them to enjoy reading and to get something from what they read. What's the use of reading if you don't enjoy it or can't understand what you've read? Lots of them came into first grade already knowing their letters, and a few can already read some words or even simple books. It's my job to make sure they understand what it's all about. I want them to be able to understand what they're reading, and we work hard at it.*

Certainly, I thought, the instructional practices of the classroom could not be responsible for Amy's "mistaken" perception.

My next thought was that perhaps Amy, at age six, was simply confused about reading. After all, some early research in the field of reading looked at children's perceptions and concluded that beginning readers focus on decoding and fail to see reading as a meaning-gaining activity. It was also suggested that their understandings of reading are limited, incomplete, and sometimes inaccurate (Baker & Brown, 1984; Bondy, 1985; Johns, 1972, 1974; Mayfield, 1983; Oliver, 1975; Reid, 1966; Weintraub & Denny, 1965).

For the most part, however, these studies were conducted by asking children a set of questions, such as "What is reading?" and quantifying their answers within predetermined categories—for example, vague (e.g., "I don't know"), object-related (e.g., "Helps you learn things"), value terms (e.g., "Reading is good"), mechanical descriptions (e.g., "It's words and you sound them out"), and meaning (e.g., "Knowing what the story is about"). Many of the studies had been conducted over relatively brief periods of time and required first-graders to provide on-the-spot answers to the researchers' queries.

I had always felt that these studies could be enriched, as in my experience as a teacher and a researcher I knew that it sometimes takes days, weeks, or even months of observing and talking to beginning readers before one can begin to connect and grasp the true meaning of what they are saying. I also felt that, by imposing adult categories (e.g., vague) on children's views, these studies often missed the opportunity to view reading through the eyes of the child. Nonetheless, here was Amy with a response that many adults would consider to be "confused or mistaken."

But Amy seemed so bright and articulate to me. She couldn't be confused. After all, she did remark that she *"used to think reading was making sense of a story."* There seemed to be no confusion here but, rather, a transformation.

Amy's perception of reading had shifted from being meaning-oriented to being letter-oriented. Why? How?

Perhaps the key to understanding Amy was to look at how the perceptions and transformations came to be. How could Amy's understanding of reading have shifted from the meaning orientation that the school district, teacher, and basal reading program all claimed they advocated for beginning readers, to a fragmented letter orientation, which, when taken literally, demonstrates little understanding of the reading process?

A FIRST-GRADE TEACHER REMEMBERS

As a former first-grade teacher, I felt that children came to school with a great deal of prior knowledge about reading. I agreed with the body of literature, including the work of Harste, Woodward, and Burke; Graves; Goodman; Smith; and others, that argues that children make sense of their world of reading and enter school as accomplished language learners who would view reading as a meaning-oriented activity.

But as a researcher, I could not disregard what Amy had reported. Amy clearly stated that she had come to understand that reading was "now…just letters." I began thinking about my own first-grade teaching experiences, and an uneasiness began to color my remembrances. Yes, I was able to recall quite readily the many children who would spontaneously talk to me about their favorite books, apparently with a deep understanding of stories, but I also recalled how some of my students at times seemed to be totally immersed and preoccupied in learning the mechanical aspects of reading, such as letter names and letter sounds. I began to remember, too, how some children would become so concerned about completing workbook pages and skill sheets that they would exhibit little interest in or devote little time to the actual stories they read.

I even began to remember how I, too, had sometimes become caught up in the mechanics of instruction. There were always so many stories left in the basal to get through by winter vacation, or so many workbook pages to complete before it was time for the end-of-the-year testing. I recalled how much emphasis was placed on each child finishing the year "on grade level" in first grade. These pressures were imposed by myself as well as others as I became more and more cautious of the curriculum, supervisors, parents, and perhaps even those second-grade teachers who expressed great concern when children came to second grade not having completed the first-grade skills curriculum.

The more I remembered of my early first-grade teaching experiences, in light of what I was observing in first-grade classrooms now, the more I could see how children like Amy could have perceptions of reading that were inconsistent with what an adult might expect, yet were still cogent. Undoubtedly, a great deal of decontextualized reading instruction occurs in many first-grade classrooms, which could be viewed as contradictory to a meaning-oriented understanding of reading.

I also began to remember the parents of my first-graders, especially the more anxious ones who wanted to be sure that their child was not falling behind or, more commonly, to be certain that their child was getting "ahead." They, too, seemed to feel pressured and often expressed concern about how their child was working—on what page, in what book, in what group. Some first-grade parents were often extremely anxious about how their child was "measuring up" as compared to other first-graders. They often indicated that their child's performance was indeed a reflection of their own. They often wanted concrete materials, such as workbooks or flashcards, that they could use at home to increase performance. These parents were also concerned with letters and sounds and the concrete, measurable components of reading instruction. They, too, at times seemed to think—or at least conveyed that they thought—that reading was just letters, or perhaps that "reading" meant being placed in a certain reading group.

This is not to say that all parents contacted me regarding their child's progress. There were many parents from whom I never heard and with whom I had little contact throughout the year. Therefore, it is impossible to gauge their level of concern regarding reading or to describe how they were feeling or the types of interactions they had with their children.

Yes, Amy's comment had even begun to shed new light on some of my prior knowledge as a first-grade teacher. I continued to have difficulty viewing Amy as confused or mistaken. More and more, I was beginning to feel that Amy's comments were well founded. Especially when viewed from Amy's perspective on reading, which at present appeared to be centered around learning about letters.

It was at this point that I decided to talk with other first-grade children, like Amy, to see if they shared her understanding of reading or perhaps had different perspectives of their own. I wanted to see if other children's percep-tions about reading had become "transformed" as a result of their school experience and how those perceptions came to be. I was eager to see how first-graders thought about reading and how their parents and teachers viewed early reading acquisition as well. I also needed to immerse myself in the professional literature on children's perceptions of reading. The next two sections summa-rize a history of the research conducted on this topic.

EARLY RESEARCH

For the most part, early studies indicated that young children beginning to read were confused about the purpose and nature of the reading task (Reid, 1966; Francis, 1973; Johns, 1972). As a result of these investigations, researchers' attention began to focus on the child's view of reading and learning to read.

Vernon (1957), in a study of low-achieving readers, was one of the first to conclude that young children are in a state of cognitive confusion when presented with the task of learning to read. This theory was widely accepted and supported by research that further investigated children's understanding of print through the use of interviews with young children.

For example, in 1963, Denny and Weintraub began an inquiry in five first-grade classrooms in three school districts to investigate students' perceptions of reading. Interviews were conducted individually with 111 first-grade students. Responses to three specific questions ("Do you want to learn how to read?" "Why?" "What must you do to learn how to read in first grade?") were taped, analyzed, and classified into predetermined categories. Denny and Weintraub (1966) concluded, "A fourth of all these entering first graders could express no logical, meaningful purpose for learning to read and a third of these children had no idea how it was accomplished" (p. 447).

Additionally, Weintraub and Denny (1965) examined 108 first-graders' responses to the question, "What is reading?" The investigation revealed that 27 percent of the responses were vague (e.g., "I don't know"); 33 percent were object-related (e.g., "when you read a book"); and 20 percent characterized reading as a cognitive task (e.g., "helps you learn things"). The remaining responses were almost equally apportioned across the following categories: (1) value terms (e.g., "I think reading is a good thing to do"); (2) mechanical descriptions (e.g., "It's words and you sound them out if you don't know them"); and (3) expectations (e.g., "It's something you have to learn how to do"). Denny and Weintraub concluded that first-graders enter school with perceptions of reading that vary greatly, and they highlighted the fact that many were unable to articulate a comprehensible perception of reading.

Further, Reid (1966) conducted individual interviews three times over the course of a school year with twelve 5-year-old students and concluded that most students were aware that they could not read and had little understanding of the reading process. As did previous researchers, Reid indicated that this general vagueness regarding the reading process may interfere with students' reading progress and that a conscious effort to develop an awareness of what reading is might make a substantial difference in learning to read.

Later, Downing (1970) replicated the study of 5-year-olds that had previously been done by Reid (1966). However, he introduced some concrete stimuli to replace the somewhat abstract questions used in Reid's study. For example, he supplied the children with actual pictures, such as pictures of a person reading and of toy buses with different route numbers. This study helped to substantiate Reid's findings and concluded that beginning readers experienced difficulty in determining the purpose of reading and had only a vague understanding of how one reads.

Mason (1967) also examined students' perceptions of reading by employing the interview technique used by Reid. Unlike the students in the Reid and

Downing studies, preschoolers in the Mason study believed they could already read. Mason concluded that this finding may be due in part to the younger age of the children involved in the study. He further concluded that "one of the first steps in learning to read is learning that one doesn't already know" (p. 132) and that students do not understand what reading is.

Oliver (1975) found that for a sample of Native American children, most 4-year-olds linked reading with behaviors such as "blowing the nose," "putting on glasses," and "just looking" (p. 868). Results indicated although 5-year-olds demonstrated some knowledge of reading, most did not associate reading with meaning and "generally seemed to lack a clear concept of written language as coded speech, and generally seemed to think of reading and writing as something they will learn to do 'when they get bigger' " (p. 869).

Johns and Ellis (1976) conducted one of the largest studies of this type, interviewing 1,655 students in grades 1 through 8. The following questions were asked and later classified into predetermined categories:

1. What is reading?
2. What do you do when you read?
3. If someone didn't know how to read, what would you tell them they need to know?

Johns and Ellis concluded that the majority of children were unaware of the reading process, although older children had a better understanding of reading than did younger childen. They also found that most children described reading as a decoding, task-oriented process rather than as a search for meaning.

The aforementioned studies are but a few of the many works that have suggested that young children have a very limited and often confused understanding of reading. In an extensive literature review of over one hundred studies, Yaden (1984) concluded that the studies that dealt with "concepts about the nature, purposes and processes of reading" reported that beginning readers failed to see reading as a meaning-related activity. He stated:

> Indeed most studies indicated that the majority of students could provide no intelligible description at all. Most other children viewed reading within the confines of a school-related task like learning the alphabet, doing workbook pages, or retelling stories to the teacher. (p. 14)

It must be noted, however, that these studies for the most part utilized direct questioning and imposed "adult" definitions on children's responses. The topics were not initiated by the children. Instead, the research agenda was to examine what the child said in relation to what an adult expected.

RECENT STUDIES

More recent studies (Dahlgren & Olsson, 1986; Michel, 1990; Swanson, 1985; Weiss & Hagen, 1988) suggest that children's perceptions of reading are not limited or confused but, on the contrary, are important in better understanding the reading process. These studies indicate that confusion and emotional pressures might be avoided if teachers and other adults considered children's perceptions of reading as important as their own perceptions (Dahlgren & Olsson, 1986).

As early as 1969, Downing proposed that teachers might begin instruction with the child's perceptions of reading by "adapting the demands of the adult world to the natural development of their pupils" (p. 230). These thoughts have been further advanced more recently by Long, Manning, and Manning (1985) as they advocated collecting data concerning the child's perceptions of print and using that information as a "basis for determining appropriate instruction" (p. 9).

Swanson (1985) advanced the importance of children's perceptions as an instructional tool as she concluded, "the thought that students may not perceive the intent of instruction has great implications for improving teacher effectiveness" (p. 123).

Through observing children and listening to their perceptions of reading, teachers can create students' literacy experiences from a framework that the child already understands, increasing the probability of reading success. This concept of informal, naturalistic observation as an effective way to learn about language and learning has been coined as "kidwatching" and is the major focus of the book *Observing the Language Learner,* edited by Angela Jaggar and M. Trika Smith-Burke. Jaggar and Smith-Burke (1985) help us understand the importance of observation and listening to children:

> The key to effective teaching is building on what students have already learned. The best way to discover this is to listen and watch closely as children use language—spoken and written—in different settings and circumstances. Careful observations over time will reveal individual styles and patterns of language use. As patterns emerge, teachers can reflect on them, comparing information to past observations and to their knowledge of language development, to determine what their students know (competence) and can do (skill) with language. When combined with informed reflection, observation becomes inquiry (Amarel, 1980); that is, careful study which leads to sound judgments about children, and to continual learning for the teacher. (p. 5)

Longitudinal, observational research that has examined children's literacy behaviors and explanations of their reading and writing (Harste, Woodward, & Burke, 1984) and provided anecdotal accounts of children's descriptions of their own reading and writing behaviors (Calkins, 1983, 1986) has provided us with a better understanding of how children learn to read and write. These studies, however, were primarily interested in exploring how children learn the functions of language and acquire skill in using language to communicate, to think, and to learn, rather than in understanding the children's point of view about their learning.

The research cited in this discussion has provided the foundation of knowledge necessary to conceptualize and implement an investigation specifically designed to study children's perceptions of reading. As research methodologies and attitudes change, we are able to look at children's perceptions in new ways. For example, as discussed earlier, Oliver (1975) concluded that children had little knowledge of reading because of comments linking reading with behaviors such as "putting on glasses." If a child had the opportunity to explain the relationship between "putting on glasses" and reading, or a researcher observed this relationship as it was taking place, the researcher would be less likely to conclude that the child was confused.

Mason (1967) found that preschoolers believed they could read. Mason concluded that these children must *discover* that they do not already know how to read. A very different conclusion would likely be reached today, based on the same data, by those who adhere to an emergent literacy philosophy. Harste, Burke, and Woodward (1981) discuss a transition they went through while conducting a qualitative study.

> We began our study of what 3, 4, 5, and 6-year old children know about written language with a good deal of optimism, assured that they know much more about print than what teachers and beginning reading and writing programs assume. What the results of our efforts have taught us is that we began not being optimistic enough; that children know much more than we or past researchers have ever dared assume, and that many of the premises and assumptions with which we began must give way to a more generous perspective if research and understanding are to proceed. (p. 2)

As it becomes more prevalent for reading researchers to "immerse themselves in classroom or home reading activities, observe the participants' words and actions, record their interactions, and then examine these records to locate patterns of communication and behavior that might provide insight into how participants make sense of social situations" (Shannon, 1989, xviii), and if as a result we better understand how perceptions evolve, then it is only natural that our conclusions may be different as we continue to add to what we have already learned from existing research. It is important to note the paradigm shift in some of the more recent research. Instead of examining the relationship between what a child says and what an adult expects, it has become important to some to understand reading from the child's perspective.

In order to understand and value children's perceptions of reading as valid information that can help us as teachers and researchers, we must be ready and willing to listen to the children as they talk during the school day. There is a perfect example of what I mean in Beverly Cleary's novel *Ramona the Pest*. Listen to Ramona as she talks to her teacher after hearing the story of *Mike Mulligan and his Steam Shovel*, by Virginia Lee Burton:

"Miss Binney, I want to know—how did Mike Mulligan go to the bathroom when he was digging the basement of the town hall?"

Miss Binney's smile seemed to last longer than smiles usually last. Ramona glanced uneasily around and saw that others were waiting with interest for the answer. Everybody wanted to know how Mike Mulligan went to the bathroom.

"Well—" said Miss Binney at last. "I don't really know, Ramona. The book doesn't tell us."

"I always wanted to know, too," said Howie, without raising his hand, and others murmured in agreement. The whole class, it seemed, had been wondering how Mike Mulligan went to the bathroom.

"Maybe he stopped the steam shovel and climbed out of the hole he was digging and went to a service station," suggested a boy named Eric.

"He couldn't. The book says he had to work as fast as he could all day," Howie pointed out. "It doesn't say he stopped."

Miss Binney faced the twenty-nine earnest members of the kindergarten, all of whom wanted to know how Mike Mulligan went to the bathroom.

"Boys and girls," she began, and spoke in a clear, distinct way. "The reason the book does not tell us how Mike Mulligan went to the bathroom is that it is not an important part of the story. The story is about digging the basement of the town hall, and that is what the book tells us."

Miss Binney spoke as if this explanation ended the matter, but the kindergarten was not convinced. Ramona knew and the rest of the class knew that knowing how to go the bathroom *was* important. They were surprised that Miss Binney did not understand, because she had showed them the bathroom the very first thing. Ramona could see there were some things she was not going to learn in school, and along with the rest of the class she stared reproachfully at Miss Binney.

The teacher looked embarrassed, as if she knew she had disappointed her kindergarten. (pp. 16–17)*

* Reprinted by permission from *Ramona the Pest* by Beverly Cleary, copyright © 1968 by William Morrow and Company, Inc., New York.

Today's Miss Binney, one hopes, would recognize this discussion not as cause for embarrassment but as a wonderful opportunity not only for creative problem solving and divergent thinking, but also for finding out what was on the minds of the children in her class. Ramona was able to tell her teacher exactly what *was* important to the children; whenever this happens, we cannot afford to conclude that, because it is unimportant to *us*, the children must be mistaken, confused, or off track.

Whenever children talk to us, we have choices in terms of responding. We can refute the children's statement: "It is not an important part of the story" (p. 17). Or we can ignore them and avoid dealing with their questions or comments: "She recovered quickly, closed the book, and told the class that if they would walk quietly to the playground she would teach them a game called Gray Duck" (pp. 17–18). This tactic will virtually ensure that before long the children will have less and less to contribute other than what is already in the teacher's mind or in the answer key of the teacher's manual. Finally, we could show that we appreciate their insights and probe to find out more of their ideas. We learn from them, little as they are, and modify our instruction on the basis of what they have taught us.

THE CHILD'S PERSPECTIVE

The research presented in this book does not focus on an adult perspective of reading. Rather, it attempts to describe reading totally from the point of view of the child and thus advances a child-driven definition of reading. This research is founded on the belief that the child's perspective is critical to understanding how children learn to read.

Recent research indicates that simply by virtue of living, the child has built up a great understanding of literacy (Templeton, 1986). By listening carefully to what children say about reading and observing what they do when they read, adults can understand things about emergent reading that we can learn in no other way. To understand the children's behavior, we must understand their definitions and the process by which these are constructed. Bogdan (1982) explains that reading "can only be understood by looking at the interplay between how people come to define reading in the specific situations in which they find themselves" (pp. 7–8). That is, there is no one definition of reading which can account for the complexity of the various social situations. Many researchers (Harste, Woodward, & Burke, 1984; Teale, 1984) emphasize the social aspect of literacy. Through interaction, the individual constructs meaning (Becker, Geer, Hughes, & Strauss, 1961), and reading comes to be defined differently in each setting. Such a view is represented in the symbolic interactionist tradition of social science research.

The term *symbolic interactionism* was coined in 1937 by Herbert Blumer (1969, p. 1), who describes three premises basic to symbolic interactionism:

> ...human beings act toward things on the basis of the meanings that things have for them...the meaning of such things is derived from, or arises out of, the social interaction that one has with one's fellows,...these meanings are handled in, and modified through, an interpretative process used by the person in dealing with the things he encounters. (p. 2)

The importance of social meaning suggests a research methodology that helps us understand the world from the perspective of an individual or a particular group of individuals.

In my study of first-graders, which will be discussed and referred to throughout this book, data-gathering techniques such as participant observation, in-depth interviewing, and document analysis were used in order to discover meaning as children see it and to build theory inductively from the experiences represented by these data (e.g., Blumer, 1969; Bogdan, 1982; Bogdan & Biklen, 1982; Glaser & Strauss, 1967).

In order to observe how reading is experienced by students, it was necessary for me to make myself a part of the classroom environment. The process of children's socialization in a particular classroom involves the development of attitudes and beliefs about their world and themselves. The study of such intensive and ongoing interaction within one single classroom results in the development of a picture of its internal order and logic (Becker, 1970). I felt that it was critical for me to achieve this in-depth understanding, and so elected to pursue, as Becker suggests, a detailed study of first-graders. Participant observation allowed me to engage in "prolonged periods of intense social interaction" with those being studied, "during which time data, in the form of field notes, are being unobtrusively and systematically collected" (Bogdan, 1972).

Qualitative research, specifically symbolic interaction, permitted me to study how children think about reading and how the various contexts in which literacy events occur influence children's perceptions. I studied reading through the point of view of the child, and, through this perspective, I have come to understand how Amy and other first-graders think about reading and about themselves as readers.

A Classroom Teacher Responds...

Do I view reading and teaching "through the eyes of children"? I know that my views on reading and teaching have changed dramatically over the years, but I wonder if my perceptions do match those of the children I teach. This chapter arouses my interest and my curiosity. I would like to find ways that I can focus more on what and how my children think.

The statement that Amy made—"I used to think reading was making sense of a story, but now I know it's just letters"—makes me shudder. I know I have been guilty, over the years, of turning the act of reading into a complicated letter/sound endeavor. But for the most part, my approach to the teaching of reading is holistic and meaningful. I don't believe the author is suggesting that I necessarily change my teaching approach but, rather, that I might add a new dimension to my instruction. This chapter recommends that I listen more actively to what my children have to say about reading, try to determine what they perceive as meaningful reading activities, and continually examine whether the reading program is meaningful and important.

The research portion of this chapter is thought-provoking. As a teacher and a parent of two young children, I concur with the research perspective that advances that preschool children enjoy many meaningful reading experiences. They love books, are able to relate a story's message to their own experiences, and are rarely bothered by not knowing a word or concept. As a teacher, I often wonder why young school-aged children lose their love and desire to read. I am concerned that previous research finds young children viewing reading as isolated letters, workbook pages, and teacher-directed tasks. I know I try to make reading instruction meaningful and fun, but I also understand the pressure to teach skills and cover so many books by the end of the school year. Accountability is inevitable, and it is always on my mind as a teacher.

The findings of the more recent research suggest that the process of finding out what a child already understands and has learned will help me as I begin formal reading instruction. The idea of delving deeper into the child's perspective may improve my teaching, thus enhancing student learning.

I can't help but find myself eager to understand how my children view reading. I want to learn more about the techniques the author used in interviewing the students. Perhaps if I can view reading from a child's perspective, I will be better equipped to teach that child not only to read, but to love reading.

Parents Respond...

As parents of three very different children, we are not surprised that first-graders have a range of perceptions of reading. Any perception must, of course, be a snapshot in time, colored by a child's experiences and stage of development. It follows that a child's perceptions can vary widely over time. Furthermore, a child can be expected to describe reading in his or her own language. The first-graders in this study, as do many children at this age, describe all kinds of things in ways that perplex adults and even make us chuckle. Their descriptions, as evidenced by the many quotations in this text, can be vivid, precise, or seemingly off-the-wall. This remains true at our home, as we think of the variety of ways our children describe a friend, relate what they did at a birthday party, or tell about their latest class field trip.

As we think about it, we've seen our three children go through a number of stages as they come to grips with reading:

- The initial focus is on the pictures in bedtime story-books such as *Goodnight Moon*. Their first interaction with the page is figuring out what everything is in the pictures. They seem to listen to the words as keys to help them unlock the mysteries of the pictures.
- Later the attention turns to the story as told in the words of favorite books. This results in their being able to tell the story back to the parent (often verbatim). Our children at this point would tell us that they were reading.
- Then the focus seems to change again, as they realize each word on the page has significance. The decoding process begins—usually with recognition of individual letters.
- They soon learn to seek clues in figuring out whole words—clues from pictures, from the context, from sounding out words, from whole word memorization/recognition. They naturally try a variety of tricks to help them.
- From this intense focus on words there eventually emerges a shift to meaning and the bigger picture again.
- At this point our children seem to realize that reading gives them a new power that allows them to participate in an "adult" world. Suddenly every street sign is read out loud triumphantly!

The details of the learning process described here have differed for each of our children depending on the rate of their development, whether the child was the oldest or had older siblings, and what they did in nursery school. But sooner or later, they all seemed to go through the steps mentioned above.

We haven't thought much before about how reading is actually taught in the classroom. Yes, as parents we see worksheets, readers, and other "evidence" of the process, but we have never really inquired about the process itself. As long as it appeared that our children were making progress and we were told they were doing O.K., we were satisfied.

This chapter has major implications for everyone involved in our entire educational system. Listening to children and tailoring instruction to what they tell us takes lots of personal attention. Can this be done effectively with thirty-plus children in a classroom? Can teachers keep fresh and enthusiastic year after year with such demands on their time? What role can parents play in helping their children learn?

For us, this chapter also implies that ongoing dialogue between parents and teachers is critical to understanding children and mutually guiding their progress. With that in mind, as parents, we would applaud those first-grade teachers who focus the agenda for parent–teacher conferences to stimulate meaningful dialogue. At times, conferences for our children have been superficial and general chit-chat. As long as the goal is a mutual better understanding of the needs of our children and of the children themselves, conferences can be a powerful tool to enhance learning.

▶ 2

The Study:
Listening Questions

PREVIEW

This chapter will introduce you to the first-grade children who participated in this study. It will also present the research methodology utilized and expose you to one of the most critical concepts of this book, listening questions. A sample interview is included to show how one might go about eliciting important information from young children by listening and asking questions.

After reading this chapter, I hope you will be eager to place yourself in the role of teacher-researcher. You will see that classroom teachers are placed in the ideal situation to study and learn from children. The study and listening questions described in this chapter can be used as a model for your own inquiry as you attempt to gain a better understanding of both teaching and learning.

THE CLASSROOM

My research began in a K–6 elementary school in a suburban school district in central New York. The first-grade classroom was suggested by the district superintendent as a good study site because it was a "typical" first-grade for the area. The teacher was known to be conscientious and cooperative and, according to the school principal, used "standard" instructional reading approaches. I probed the meaning of "standard" with the principal and was told that the teacher instructed the children in three small groups for reading and used basal reading materials with her students on a daily basis.

I was introduced to the teacher and, after some brief preliminary conversation, was presented to the class as Pam, "who will be visiting our classroom to see how we learn and what we do in first grade." The teacher also mentioned to the class that I would be talking to them from time to time, and she asked them to make me feel welcome.

I found the classroom to be quite structured, with a daily routine in evidence. The day's activities began with "Calendar," and the children recited the day and date in unison. Each morning someone was chosen to put a marker (a leaf in September, a pumpkin in October) on the appropriate day; when each person had had a turn, the cycle began again. After Calendar, another person's name was chosen from the wishing well to be the "star" for the day. The teacher read the name out loud and said, "Today is [Erin's] day, and we know all her wishes will come true. She is a special person whose name was picked to have a great day." The name was put on the blackboard along with the name of the designated calendar helper. The teacher would then remind the children to sit up straight because it was time to pass out their daily seatwork. She would read and explain the directions for each activity to be completed independently before lunch. After the children had received directions, she would remind them to put their names on all of the papers. As the teacher was seated in the reading corner, she would whisper, "Remember, there is no talking during reading groups. You may begin." At this time, the children would all begin their seatwork.

The teacher would call each reading group to the front of the room by using the name that the children had designated. Groups were labeled anything from Yankees to Carebears. When a group was called, five to ten children would quietly walk to the front of the classroom and sit on chairs placed in a circle. They would bring their reading books, workbooks, pencils, and sometimes supplementary ditto sheets, without being asked. The teacher also sat in the circle. Each of the three reading groups regularly received 25 to 30 minutes of instruction each morning.

Instruction typically consisted of taking turns reading orally, with coaching and correcting by the teacher; reading silently; answering questions about the story; and either completing or correcting workbook pages and worksheets. The session typically ended with the teacher assigning seatwork such as additional workbook pages to be completed independently by the children when they returned to their seats.

Reading was not confined to the reading group, as the children were exposed to reading tasks and instruction throughout the day. For instance, the whole class often participated in an activity where the children would take turns reading orally. A child would stand up and begin reading and was permitted to read until he or she made a mistake, at which time the child was required to sit down again. The children also wrote and read stories several times a week in the afternoon, and their teacher read to them after playtime on a regular basis.

After six months of interviewing and doing participant observation in one first-grade classroom, I felt it would be useful to study additional classrooms with different children, teachers, and instructional approaches. This type of sample selection is referred to as theoretical sampling, as described by Glaser and Strauss (1967). That is, I selected the teachers, their classes, and parents for their apparent ability to answer questions that emerged as data were collected, and I began to identify further questions that needed to be pursued in my study. I spoke with the district reading coordinator, who suggested interviewing the children and teachers in two classrooms that incorporated instructional practices that were not quite as "standard" as the classroom I had been studying thus far. That is, the teachers in these classrooms, although they used instructional groups for reading, were much less dependent on the basal readers for primary reading instruction. In addition to the basal reading program, they incorporated a great deal of independent reading throughout the day. Language experience activities and story writing were integrated into the ongoing reading program. The instruction in both of these classrooms was perceived by the reading coordinator to be considerably less structured and did not focus on mastery of specific skills, as it did the classroom I initially studied.

My observations and interviews found the reading coordinator's perceptions to be quite accurate. In fact, one of the classrooms I observed was for the most part basal-independent and relied primarily on holistic language learning experiences in order to develop reading acquisition.

It was apparent that the instructional approaches utilized in these two additional first grades were different from those used in the classroom I had been observing initially. Observing and interviewing the children in these additional classrooms made it possible to understand better how, if at all, instructional practices influenced children's understanding of reading. At this point, I was observing and interviewing an additional fifty-three students.

The children involved in this study were from a variety of socioeconomic levels and physical locations within the district, and represented a range of ability levels. Overall, the children in this study could be described as lower- to middle-class suburban youngsters who came from both working-class and professional homes.

Early in the study, it became apparent that many of the children were making a distinction between reading at home and reading in school. Remarks were made that evidenced distinctively different understandings of reading in the two contexts, such as, "Reading at home is when my sister and I look at books, and reading at school is getting my work done."

To understand better how the children viewed reading both at home and at school, I decided to interview the families of some of the first-graders with whom I had talked. Nine families agreed to be interviewed. A note describing the study was sent home by the principal, and the families who volunteered to participate in the study were contacted. The interviews were conducted in their homes. I talked to mothers, fathers, grandparents, brothers, and sisters, and I witnessed what the children meant when they talked about reading at home.

Each family was interviewed in their own home in an attempt to make the members more comfortable and to allow me to observe families in their natural environment. This enabled me to become more a part of the children's home life, as I was often invited to meals and parties and became involved in activities where reading took place.

DATA COLLECTION

I conducted participant observations in the initial first-grade classroom three to five times per week from September through March, as well as in the two additional classrooms over a four-week period in February and March. As data were collected, field notes and important documents were examined, and observer's comments were written to note emerging themes, to speculate on patterns and relationships, and to examine my role in each given setting

(Bogdan & Biklen, 1982). Documents examined included reading directives from administration, notes sent to teachers from the principal, letters that the teachers sent home, information on district policy and curricula, and memoranda from meetings.

Analysis of data was ongoing and continued throughout the study. I developed categories, interpretations, and hypotheses from the field notes in an attempt to discover where my data were weak and where my observations and interviews needed to be focused in the future. In early April, when little new material had been discovered for some time, I stopped data collection for several weeks. By that time, the data obtained from both observation and interviews concerning children's perceptions of reading could be more or less predicted; that is, no new categories emerged. Data were then sorted and re-sorted into categories and subcategories. Interview transcripts, field notes, and important documents were read carefully to develop general topic codes such as "children's perceptions of reading." I then marked each appropriate line or section with the code in the margin and filed each section according to the appropriate code. Within each of the more general categories (e.g., children's perceptions of reading) were a number of subcategories (e.g., task, process, purpose) that were color-coded, the goal being to identify themes and make hypotheses (Bogdan & Biklen, 1982). Once these categories were established, they provided the necessary framework from which to better understand children's perceptions of reading. To test my preliminary hypotheses generated from these categories, I went back in May for informal interviews with the same children.

Throughout the school year I also spent time in other settings such as lunchrooms, monthly meetings of the Parent–Teacher Association, field trips, libraries, faculty rooms, and the school playground. At an early point during my observations at home and school, I began to realize that children could readily articulate their perceptions of reading as well as describe the differences between reading at home and at school. This realization was a critical decision point, which led to my desire to give credence to what the children said by reporting it. These articulations may not represent all that the children know and act upon, but they are nonetheless powerful representations of the children's awareness. Rather than providing detailed description of children's print-related behaviors both at home and at school, I chose to use participant observations in an effort to access the compelling stories children had to tell.

Open-ended interviews were conducted throughout the study with both the teachers and the children in the classrooms; they extended as well to administrators, special service staff, parents, and siblings. The interviews gave me additional insight and provided me the opportunity to periodically rephrase my developing interpretations as questions for comment. This procedure allowed me to match my explanation against those of the participants in the study. The interview questions focused on many emerging themes and helped me make sense of what I observed during participant observation. Because I had the opportunity to talk to the teachers and the children often, over an extended period of time, I was able to build the rapport necessary to uncover information that they might otherwise have been reluctant to reveal. More important, sustained dialogue helped me to discover what questions to pursue, because in such relaxed situations people often choose to talk about what is most important to them. I could address remarks that children initiated and probe for details.

The circumstances of the particular observation or interview determined whether I took field notes or taped at the actual time of inquiry. In a few cases the children, parents, teachers, or administrators asked not to be taped; occasionally, I made the judgment not to tape or take notes if it seemed to be interfering with the quality of the interview. When recording or writing was not possible, field notes were written immediately following the interaction so that the experiences were reconstructed as accurately as possible. Field notes were written for each observation and attempted to represent events as precisely as possible. As data were being collected, I also wrote observer's comments to note emerging themes and to examine my role in a given setting.

All interviews of children were either taped and transcribed or written verbatim. I attempted to establish relationships with the children based on mutual trust and respect. When I first met a child, I would generally explain that I wanted to write a book about reading and that I was very interested in what children thought and did. I further explained that I needed help from children to write this book and that, in fact, I couldn't write it without their assistance.

When I entered the children's classroom, home, playground, or other setting, I would take my cues from them. If they wanted to swing, I would swing. If they wanted to read, I would read. Often, the children would talk to me as we were involved in various activities. It became clear to me that the children would often ask me to participate in activities such as coloring to test the relationship. As one 6-year-old girl said after we had colored at least ten pictures, "All right, I would like to help you write that book."

The children began to treat me differently than they did other adults at home or school. I really didn't fit any of the "adult-types" they knew (e.g., teacher, principal, custodian, parent, relative). One 6-year-old remarked, "You don't seem like most grown-ups. You seem like a big kid. Maybe it's because you don't have a job." They began to confide their thoughts and to preface remarks by telling me that this was something they wanted me to know, but it was not to be shared with their teacher.

The children came to expect me to show up and would be upset if I had to miss certain occasions such as important soccer games, concerts, or parties. I had definitely become part of their everyday lives. After I returned from being sick for a day, one child said, "We were wondering where you were yesterday. Lots of us had things to tell you for the book."

LISTENING QUESTIONS

It is very important to note that the children often did not respond to direct questions. Many first-graders began the interaction by responding, "I don't know," to questions like, "What is reading?" When further examined, the response, "I don't know," often meant, "I don't feel like talking about this"; "My friends are playing, and I want to play, too"; or "I haven't thought about it and I need more time." The words "I don't know" cannot be interpreted literally and are not indicative of what a child truly knows about reading—nor is any single response an indication of all a child has come to understand about the reading process.

This research relied heavily on in-depth interviews with first-graders as a data-gathering technique. Unlike many earlier studies on children's perceptions, I had no predetermined interview schedule or set of questions to be asked. The interviews conducted were open-ended in nature. Indeed, my interviews with first-graders resembled informal conversations far more than formal interviews with their accompanying questions and answers.

My primary agenda during my interaction with a first-grader was to listen and attempt to understand. It is not that I never asked questions. My field notes show that questions were a major element of much of my interaction with the children. My field notes also reveal, however, that the questioning technique I used was far different from that described in most studies. I seldom asked direct questions of first-graders. Instead, the questions I asked were usually indirect and more often than not did not resemble questions at all. I questioned children in half sentences ("What else?"), with single words ("Easy?"), with encouraging laughter, and with affirming glances, and even body posture.

Sometimes I purposely asked nothing, as when I sat on the swing beside Marcus, a shy 6-year-old whom I had been observing all week during reading group. We simply swung for ten minutes or so, saying nothing until his teacher called the class in from playtime. "Thanks for letting me swing with you," was my only utterance. Two days later, Marcus, with shy, down-turned eyes, quietly approached me in a free reading corner with his new library book and announced, "I can read this book." That day I listened to Marcus read and tell me about reading for a full twenty minutes before it was time for lunch. That was the only time he "opened up," but I don't think that interview would have taken place had we not swung in silence two days earlier.

Other times I engaged in a straightforward spirited give-and-take with a first-grader, as when Ellen walked by my chair and I stopped her with, "Hey, Ellen, what have you got there?" "My workbook," she replied, to which I countered, "What do you do in that?" That was enough to start a focused dialogue, which revealed among other things that Ellen thought that workbooks were "dumb" and that *she* wished *she* could just read books as she did at home when *she* went to bed.

More often than not, direct questions ("What is reading?") were met with imprecise answers ("I don't know," "You know," or "It's hard"). Other times a direct question received a nonanswer, which would generally take the form of turned-down eyes, an uneasy smile, or perhaps the beginnings of a frightened tremor. The imprecise responses almost inevitably could be transformed into a meaningful interaction by proceeding cautiously, with sensitivity, and by listening. Take, for instance, Marsha, who, when asked, "Tell me about reading," simply looked in another direction and mumbled, "I don't know." My response was to say nothing and pick up a *Curious George* book from the shelf. I silently began turning pages until Marsha gazed slowly and cautiously toward the book. I paused at a page, pointed a finger at Curious George, and uttered a reserved laugh. I now had Marsha's attention and was ready to try again. "Funny book," I said. "Uh huh," Marsha whispered under her breath. "Ever read this book?" I asked. "Uh huh. Do ya like it?" Marsha asked as she snuggled next to me on the chair. "Know any other books?" I asked. "I can read my own books at home but not in school," Marsha blurted out. The interview had begun! Approximately ten minutes later we ended our conversation, and I immediately began writing, trying to capture all that Marsha had revealed about reading.

Most of my interviews do include some questions. Hundreds of pages of field notes suggest, however, that the most productive questions are often the least direct; in general, the fewer the questions, the richer the interview. Responses can be followed by abbreviated, affirming comments from the interviewer, such as "Ahh," or "That's interesting," and the child should do the majority of the talking. I call this style of interviewing using "listening questions." The objective is to have a conversation and be a good listener, rather than to conduct a question-and-answer exchange. The interviewer is not merely acquiring answers but also learning what questions are important to ask and how to ask them. I believe this is the key to understanding children.

The following interview is one of the many interviews I conducted in my research that exemplifies the "listening question" style.

Setting—Free Reading Corner

Interviewer: (Smiling) Hi, Mike. What are you up to today?

Mike: (He says nothing.)

Interviewer: I saw your drawing on the bulletin board.

Mike: Yuh?

Interviewer: I drew this one. (Brings out a drawing of a cockeyed cat.)

Mike: (Moves closer to look at the drawing and laughs.)

Interviewer: (Hands pencil to Mike.) Maybe he needs a collar.

Mike: (Takes pencil and draws collar on cat.) Here.

Interviewer: Hey! That looks good, Mike. You must like to draw.

Mike: Yeah. But I like to use colored markers. Mrs. Craig lets us paint sometimes. That's what I like best 'cuz you get to use big paper and take it home.

Interviewer: What do you do with your pictures when you take them home?

Mike: Sometimes my Mom puts it on the refrigerator, or I work on it with her or Karen.

Interviewer: Who's Karen?

Mike: My sister.

Interviewer: Your sister?

Mike: Yeah. She's in third grade.

Interviewer: Does she like to draw?

Mike: Yeah. She draws lots of stuff. Even stories.

Interviewer: Stories?

Mike: Yeah. Like if the cat had a story.

Interviewer: Like what?

Mike: (Long pause) Like if the cat said something. (Silence) Yeah. You know if the words told what the cat said.

Interviewer: You mean...?

Mike: Yeah. If the cat said, "I want some food."

Interviewer: Oh! I get it. Like, if I wrote, "I want some food." (Takes marker and prints under the picture of the cat.)

Mike: Yeah. Like that.

Interviewer: Can you read that?

Mike: (Hesitates and stares at the sheet.) I'm hungry gimme some food.

Interviewer: Hey, that's good reading. Do you read a lot?

Mike: Me and Karen read sometimes.

Interviewer: Your sister?

Mike: Yeah.

Interviewer: How?

Mike: Like when she writes stories, or if I read one of my books and she helps me read sometimes.

Interviewer: Helps you?

Mike: If I don't know a word or something she helps me read it.

Interviewer: The word?

Mike: Yeah. Like she tells me to sound it out or something.

Interviewer: Ooh.

Mike: She tells me to sound it out with my finger.

Interviewer: With your finger?

Mike: Uh huh.

Interviewer: How?

Mike: Well, you know.

Interviewer: I'm not sure.

Mike: Sound it out with your finger.

Interviewer: Can you show me? (Puts cat picture in front of Mike.)

Mike: Ya have to put your finger by the word.

Interviewer: Like this? (Puts finger under the word cat.)

Mike: Uh huh. Cat.

Interviewer: Oh, I get it. Karen points to the word.

Mike: Yeah, and I sound it out. But sometimes I can't so she just tells me or something. Sometimes I'm tired, and my eyes wanna sleep.

Interviewer: Want to sleep?

Mike: Yeah. Like I'm lying on my pillow with my book, and I get tired, and then Karen just reads it, and sometimes I fall asleep.

Interviewer: So you read when it's time for bed.

Mike: Yeah, that's a good time 'cuz it's quiet, and Mom lets me and Karen go to bed later. I like to read then and so does Karen.

Interviewer: Sounds like fun. Whoops! Time for lunch. Maybe we can talk more about reading later.

Mike: O.K. (Runs off, spins around, and returns.)

Mike: Can I have this picture to take home?

Interviewer: Sure!

A careful analysis of this interview helps to identify a number of important interview principles and will better illustrate the nature of "listening questions." Initially, the interview started informally with, "Hi, Mike. What are you up to today?" Calling Mike by name seemed to involve him in the interview immediately. Also, no answer was required to the initial question, as there was no expectant pause and no pressure to tell what he was actually up to. Instead, the dialogue immediately moved on to another affirmation: "I saw your picture on the bulletin board." Now the child realizes, "She knows me and she noticed my work." A further connection is established. I then produced a drawing of my own (a not-too-good drawing). This seemed to enhance our rapport, as we now had something in common to share (the drawing). A further connection was made when I encouraged and praised Mike for drawing a collar on my cat. Now we definitely had something in common.

This may seem to be a great deal of effort simply to establish rapport, but it was time well spent, as it set the tone and allowed Mike to become more comfortable, while I began to establish a sense of where the interview might go. It is important to know that the operative word is "might." You never actually know where a listening interview is going because you are not working from a set of predetermined questions. It is my feeling that a traditional first-grade interview including standard questions would have ended rather quickly and, chances are, would have resulted in more than a few "I don't know"s.

In the next phase of the interview I deliberately led Mike into talking about his involvement in a school-related task, drawing. Reading was not yet mentioned, but I continued to focus the conversation on drawing, which later permitted Mike to change the setting from school to the home. I worked the introduction of Karen into the interview, as earlier interviews had already indicated that siblings played a significant role in learning to read. When Mike mentioned that Karen "drew stories," I repeated the word *stories* in an attempt to elicit more in the way of a response. I now was getting information that was the focus of my research.

After learning that Karen drew stories, I probed the home reading event, reading with an older sibling. It is important to note that the probes were brief and that, by this stage of the interview, Mike was doing most of the talking, and I was doing most of the listening. The end result was a description of sibling tutoring at home, with information regarding setting (on the bed), time (quiet time before bed), method (sound-it-out or whole-word), and feelings about reading ("I like to read at bedtime"). Contrast what was learned in this interview with what an interview schedule or protocol (e.g., "Do you read at home?") might yield.

Finally, it is important to note that I ended the interview with a gentle request to talk about reading again. Mike's affirmative answer enabled us to continue where we left off later on that same day. I was able to talk to Mike about what kinds of books he read at home and learned that he believed his sister taught him to read at home, which was consistent with what many other first-graders had suggested.

The key to a successful child interview is to start gently and comfortably, keeping the dialogue open-ended without leading. The questions asked should be "listening questions," with the interviewer doing as little telling as possible. Interviewers must remember that they are there to listen and, most important, to understand what is said from the child's viewpoint.

TEACHER AS RESEARCHER

To understand better how to think about children's perceptions of reading and to develop a sense of the research methodology used, imagine yourself for a moment sitting on a rug in the corner of a first-grade classroom, as I found myself doing, and imagine that Jimmy, a 6-year-old, is sitting opposite you as you talk informally about school. Eventually, the conversation turns to reading, and you ask Jimmy, "What is reading to you?" Jimmy pauses a minute to think, then responds, "Reading is math." How are you to think about the response? Is Jimmy, like Amy, confused or mistaken? Did he misunderstand the question? You hurriedly scribble down Jimmy's answer. Later that evening, while examining your field notes, you list the comment under the category "children's perceptions of reading." You study the other comments and note a similarity between Jimmy's and those of other first-graders. But now comes the complex part. What do you, the teacher-researcher, do with Jimmy's comment? How do you think about the response? What does it mean? More important, what does Jimmy mean when he says, "Reading is math"? I struggled with questions like this one as I collected and interpreted data.

The answers to the questions just posed largely depend on your perspective of the role children play in the reading environment. If you permit yourself to apply an adult interpretation to Jimmy's view, you would probably be forced to conclude that he is mistaken or confused about beginning reading instruction. If, on the other hand, you permit yourself to take a child's view of reading, and examine the comment in light of the child's social context, specifically classroom practice, you might come to a different understanding—to a conclusion that suggests that Jimmy has a rational or insightful understanding of beginning reading instruction. I have reached this conclusion after doing participant observations in three first-grade classrooms and interviewing eighty-one first-graders, parents, teachers, and school administrators in a year-long study. It is a conclusion I hope you, too, will come to embrace as you experience reading from the child's perspective in the subsequent chapters of this book.

I believe that embracing this perspective will enable you to become a more effective teacher as you begin to examine children's perceptions more carefully and adjust your instruction accordingly. You could become, in effect, both researcher and teacher as you begin to probe and act upon the child's perspective, a practice that can increase your insight and effectiveness dramatically. The succeeding chapters of the text will present information that should help you become such a teacher-researcher.

A Classroom Teacher Responds...

This chapter reinforces the fact that in order to really know my students I must establish a relaxed, safe classroom environment and be willing to spend the time to talk and listen to them. Second, honesty is an essential component in building a trusting relationship with a child. I need to be able and willing to explain to children why I teach what I do and why I expect them to work to their fullest potential.

I can't help but wonder if, in fact, instructional practices do influence a child's understanding of reading. Would the child who was asked to use a workbook that she considered "dumb" have a healthier attitude and a better reading foundation if she had been allowed to read more books? Do I throw out the workbook? Do I talk to the child about why the workbook is important? Do I modify the use of the workbook, or do I ignore the child's comment completely? How much useful information can a child provide concerning reading, and to what degree should it influence my instructional plan? These questions probably need to be answered on an individual basis, but I hope that information within this book will help my decision making.

The statement, "Reading is math," caught my attention. I wonder if Jimmy views reading as a series of pieces that, when put together, constitute a whole. I wonder if his response should be viewed as positive or negative. Jimmy's answer reminds me of the time one of my students announced that our science lesson was just like the morning's reading lesson. Jumping at the opportunity to see if I really was beginning to integrate my subject areas, I probed deeper. "How," I asked, "is our electricity lesson like the story of *Encyclopedia Brown?*" The child, shaking her head, laughed and said, "It's a mystery to me." Maybe there is a lot to be said for listening to kids!

The term *listening questions* is new to me, but it makes great sense. I think of the interest inventories I have given in an effort to know my students better and to focus instruction around their interests. These questions couldn't have been more specific—for example, "What is your favorite sport?" I now wonder: Did I assume that all children had a favorite sport, and if so, that they had only one? I think now that I gathered the information but never really did much with it.

The author's point hits home. To gather really useful information from children, one must be willing to engage in long-term conversations, provide open-ended questions, and become a very skillful listener. I am beginning to see how the art of listening can help me better understand the connections that children make as they learn. While still teaching the curriculum, I can provide myself with more insight into each child in my classroom, and, I hope, enhance the effectiveness of both teaching and learning. This is how I want to teach.

After reading Chapters 1 and 2, I now wonder: Was I responding to my own beliefs or the call of the students I taught? Did my students send me messages about what reading was to them and what it should be? As I reflect on those years, I think they did. I recall my children asking, maybe pleading, as they were asked to come to reading group, "Do we get to read today?" Such a question for a group just called to reading! But the fact was—and I knew it— that a story was read only two to three times a week because the workbook and supplemental dittos were so time-consuming. Why did it take me so long to respond to my children's plea for real reading experiences?

I know what I did to remedy my situation, and I am eager to read on...to see if some of my changes mirror the perceptions and needs of the children in this study and, I hope, to learn new ideas and strategies to implement in my classroom.

Parents Respond...

The author's contention that children have a "rational or insightful understanding of beginning reading instruction" that, when probed successfully by the teacher, can be used to guide instruction, makes good sense. We are always amazed at the range of insights our three children display—often far beyond what we would expect from children their age. The trick for us is to "read" their minds. As parents, we are continually trying all kinds of approaches to accomplish that goal, no matter what the topic. What works one day won't necessarily work the next. Direct questions sometimes work, but sometimes they don't. The probing technique that the author calls "listening questions" is an excellent one, which we believe works for us. In our household, we have even established a bedtime ritual that sets the stage for this kind of listening. Every few evenings, instead of reading a bedtime story, my wife or I will tell a true story about an experience from our childhood. This inevitably leads to a round of questions from the children. The discussion often spins off onto topics that are, at that time, important to them. In the process, we are able to steer the discussion gently in order to dig further into areas of interest and gain insight, provide advice, give guidance, or just listen.

As parents, we encourage the listener to use caution in taking one response to a question from a child too literally. A "picture" must be painted from a variety of responses. Ask the same question of a child two times in succession, and you may get two very different responses depending on the child's mood, what the child is concentrating on at the moment, and many other factors.

Listening to our children effectively is both rewarding and time-consuming. If we were teachers reading this chapter, we would ask ourselves how to find enough time during the school day to draw out students' insights on reading, math, or other areas that affect teaching and learning. We must realize that listening is essential for good instruction to take place. As we think about what we are reading, it is becoming clear that both parents and teachers must recognize that real listening is an important priority, and we must make the time available. Listening opportunities can arise spontaneously and when least expected throughout the day. We should be predisposed to seize and exploit these occasions as they occur.

▶ 3

Tasks: Circling, Underlining, and Crossing Out

PREVIEW

In this chapter you will find that when first-graders describe what reading means to them, their initial responses are typically descriptions of the tasks they are required to perform during reading instruction. You will see how reading instruction has influenced their perceptions of what reading is all about and, in many cases, has led to perceptions that appear to be confused or mistaken.

If you have read and accepted the information developed in Chapter 1, however, you will not likely view the children's responses as confused or mistaken. Instead, you will attempt to understand what the children are saying and why they are saying it. I hope this chapter will help you see how task-oriented reading instruction moves children away from meaning-oriented understandings of reading. It should also show you how you might use children's perceptions for instructional decision making.

FIRST-GRADE READING GROUPS: WHAT GOES ON

Like most reading groups, today's began with a summons from Mrs. Parks: "I'd like the Carebears to bring their chairs, workbooks, pencils, and reading books up front. Remember to do it quietly. Others are working." John searched his desk looking for something—a pencil, or perhaps his reading book. Crumpled paper after paper fell from his desk as the search continued. Finally, he grabbed a sheet of paper, stuffed it in his workbook, and scurried to the front of the room, dragging his chair as he went. John was not particularly quiet as he moved forward, but he managed to escape with little more than a stern look from Mrs. Parks and a few grumbles from classmates he bumped with his chair on the way to reading group.

The group began when Mrs. Parks asked the children to take out their word cards. John was chosen to be first. Mrs. Parks took his cards, held them up one at a time, and asked him to read each of the words. He received a sticker for each word that he read correctly and was told to practice at home the words he missed. After this procedure had been repeated with the other children, the group was directed to open their workbooks to a given page. Together the children circled, underlined, crossed out, and filled in the blanks. On the workbook page, John, like the others, was very careful not to underline more than one word, to make those circles as round as he could, and to cross out only the appropriate portion of the word. John was extra careful to finish the entire page. After completing the page, he was directed to "check his work." But John was staring blankly at the page.

The reading group session ended with Mrs. Parks explaining the reading seatwork for the day, which consisted of more circling and underlining, and an admonition for the children to go back to their seats. John scurried down the aisle, once again disturbing the children he had disrupted a mere twenty minutes before. He flopped down in his chair and started searching through his desk for something never to be found.

Later that morning, John's sister Joleen was dragging her chair to reading group in another classroom. This group started with a word hunt, where children focused their attention on a story written on chart paper in the front of the room. Each child was asked to circle a word that began with t with felt-tipped marker in their favorite color. Joleen was able to circle two words that began with *t*. After the remaining four children had circled their *t* words, the teacher directed them to remember yesterday's trip to the apple orchard. Mr. Rodriguez took a marker and wrote, "Our Visit to the Apple Orchard" on a fresh piece of white chart paper. Each child was given a turn to supply a sentence, which Mr. Rodriguez wrote verbatim on the chart paper. When the five-sentence story was completed, the children took turns reading the story, with Mr. Rodriguez helping them over the rough spots. Joleen read every word correctly except two of the words from Mark's sentence (Delicious and Wine-sap), for which Mark eagerly provided help. After reading the entire story together, the children were told to quietly return to their seats, write at least three sentences in their journals, and complete their seatwork.

In the course of the twenty to thirty minutes spent in reading group, both John and Joleen were required to execute specific directives and to perform numerous tasks stipulated by their teachers, as were the other first-graders in their classes. The tasks, though different, had a certain sameness in that the children were asked to perform specific activities, such as quietly bringing up chairs, finding and circling words, and finishing their seatwork. These tasks required John, Joleen, and the others to concentrate and focus virtually all of their energies on the task at hand. It is no wonder that when I asked children about what reading means to them, their answers were heavily laden with task descriptions.

CHILDREN'S PERCEPTIONS: TASKS

Ask a first-grader what reading means, and the first response is generally some sort of task description that describes what is done in reading at school. Interestingly, these descriptions often involve pencil-and-paper activities. As Jeff remarked, "Reading is when the teacher says circle the word or you have to put a check on it" or, as Tim commented when asked about reading, "Our teacher gives us directions about the paper and then what we do is go back to our seats and do our paper." Joshua indicated that, "Reading is when we put *X*'s on the squares and circles and sometimes we put sentences together."

Other first-graders describe reading in terms of physical tasks performed, such as, "Reading is sitting and doing work," and, "You take your books and bring them up with your pencils." Or, as Marv commented, "Reading is going up and working in your workbook or reading book." According to Andrea, "Reading is when you do ditto pages and read storybooks and workbook pages. Reading is skills tests, too. And that's about all." One first-grade girl remarked that reading is "where you stand up and sit back down." The youngster went on to explain that she would stand up to read to the class until she made a mistake or did not know a word, and then she would sit back down. Although this remark may seem outlandish, it is interesting to note that well-known reading researcher Jerry Johns (1986) documented an almost identical response when interviewing a second-grader about reading. He asked the student how he viewed reading, and the student responded, "Stand up, sit down."

Another illustration of a description of reading in terms of physical tasks was given by Stephanie, as she very deliberately explained:

> *You take your books and bring them up with your pencils. You do your papers and get reading seatwork when you are done. Then you go back to your seats. Then you go back to the paper you are working on when you're done writing your name. After that paper, you go to the next one. When you're done with those, you go on to the next one until the last one is done. Then put them in her basket. That's what reading in school is.*

Physical tasks are probably the type of task most frequently mentioned during initial conversations with first-graders. Although we cannot be entirely certain why the children so readily associate physical tasks such as circling, crossing out, underlining, and standing up and sitting down with reading, it is logical to conclude that when physical tasks predominate in reading instructional settings, children will "learn" that these tasks are equivalent to reading, or at least that this is what reading means in school.

My observations of first-grade reading groups lend credence to this theory, as I noticed that a great deal of instructional time was devoted to performing physical tasks. This is not to say that physical tasks in the name of reading instruction are always bad, given that certain physical tasks appear to be entirely necessary to beginning reading instruction. At times, first-graders must be shown how to mark an answer correctly, point with their right hand, and, yes, even walk quietly back to their seats. We must, however, constantly remind ourselves that the various physical tasks associated with beginning reading instruction have a significant impact on how children perceive reading and can often overshadow the act of reading itself. We must also recognize that these physical tasks seem to interfere with children's developing perceptions of reading as a meaning-oriented process. Engaging children in fewer physical tasks, or at least deemphasizing their importance in the reading setting, would certainly help to remedy this situation.

A number of first-graders in the study did identify reading tasks that were more text and/or story-related. Michael commented, "Reading is sort of like reading stories out of reading books and take-home books." Andrew elaborated: "Reading is books and other things. You can read newspapers when you grow up." Ryan, another first-grader, indicated that "Reading is picking out a good book to read to your mother or little sister."

Some children seem to associate reading tasks with other school tasks, particularly math. Elizabeth remarked: "Reading is math because there are new words to learn in both. We have a book for both. We come to groups and learn new words." Erin also initially "confused" reading with math but seems to have sorted the two out for herself:

When I first came to first grade, I thought reading was math. We have a board and a book and we come up with a group of kids. Now I know they're different. Reading is longer than math. Also, in reading, we read numbers and words, and in math we do just numbers. We play Bingo in both.

Curtis seemed to see a relationship between reading and math, as well. He remarked, "Reading is fun. You learn about stuff like math numbers."

This association is not surprising, as children are frequently asked to read words and sentences during math. In first grade, students learn to "make" numbers and to "make" letters. Both tasks require pencils, papers, and workbooks and responses of circling, crossing out, and coloring. As first grade progresses, the children eventually learn that numbers and letters "do" different things and serve different functions, but initially the physical tasks (and therefore perceptions) are highly connected.

The connections once again seem to be colored by instructional practices. As one first-grade teacher commented to her class while passing out reading seatwork dittos, "If you forget how to make any of your numbers or letters, you may look up at the board. They're all right up here if you need them." And, yes, the numbers and letters appeared together in the front of the room, and it seemed to be up to the children to sort out the difference between the symbols. Throughout the study, the children positioned reading and math closely in their minds.

It is clear that the school tasks performed in the name of reading instruction took on enormous importance in the minds of first-graders—so significant that task descriptions initially dominated most first-graders' responses to the question, "What is reading?" Few of the initial responses were comprehension-oriented, and few discussed reading for enjoyment, even though these appeared to be major goals of the reading program. Through months of observation, it became apparent that much of the activity in reading classes centers on reading workbooks and worksheets that require children to "do more" (or is it less?) than just reading.

During one of my classroom visits, I observed three different reading groups in which not one child was afforded the opportunity to read from a book. In fact, a book was not even part of these groups. Each group I observed plodded laboriously through twenty minutes of workbook pages, circling, underlining, and crossing out letters and pictures that made the same sounds as the letters. During these particular lessons, the teacher did not seem to be enjoying what she was doing and appeared anxious to complete the lessons. These children were not being helped to understand reading as a meaning-oriented process. The tacit message delivered in these reading groups was that reading was a physical, paper-and-pencil task. The focus of reading became not meaning-making but circling, underlining, and crossing out. In her book *In the Middle* (1987), Nancie Atwell refers to these tacit lessons as she describes "inadvertent messages" that are communicated through the standard approach to literature. Although Atwell is referring to older readers as she describes how the ways we approach literature in the secondary English classroom convey inadvertent messages to our students about reading, my research indicates that many of the same messages are being transmitted during reading instruction at the first-grade level. The following is a partial list of the tacit lessons Atwell learned as a student of literature and/or transmitted to her own students while teaching:

- Reading is difficult, serious business.
- Literature is even more difficult and serious.
- Reading is a performance for an audience of one: the teacher.
- There is one interpretation of the text: the teacher's.
- "Errors" in comprehension or interpretation will not be tolerated.
- Student readers aren't smart or trustworthy enough to choose their own texts.
- Reading requires memorization and mastery of information, terms, conventions, and theories.
- Reading is always followed by a test (and writing mostly serves to test reading—book reports, critical papers, essays, and multiple choice/fill-in-the-blank/short-answer variations).
- Reading somehow involves drawing lines, filling in blanks, and circling.
- Readers break whole texts into separate pieces to be read and dissected one fragment at a time.
- It's wrong to become so interested in a text that you read more than the fragment the teacher assigned.
- Reading is a solitary activity you perform as a member of a group.
- Readers in a group may not collaborate; this is cheating.
- Rereading a book is also cheating; so are skimming, skipping, and looking ahead.

- It's immoral to abandon a book you're not enjoying.
- You learn about literature by listening to teachers talk about it.
- Teachers talk a lot about literature, but teachers don't read.
- Teachers are often bored by the literature they want you to read.
- There's another kind of reading, a fun, satisfying kind you can do on your free time or outside of school. (pp. 152–153)*

It might be helpful to try to make explicit the tacit lessons you are demonstrating about reading, using Atwell's list as a guide. You may want to talk to the children in your classroom as you create your list. For example, discuss with them what they do when they begin reading a book and find they don't like it, or whether or not it helps them understand the stories better when you ask them questions as they are reading. Your students can be your greatest source as you try to understand what they are really learning from your teaching.

Nancie Atwell suggests that "in spite of all our heartfelt, explicit messages, the activities we sponsor and demonstrations we provide are creating too many non-readers—students who either cannot or do not read" (p. 153). I concur with Atwell as she further suggests that this is not an intended outcome. She concludes:

> We enter our classrooms determined to create readers, to do the very best we can at what we know as teachers of literature. But even the most conscientious versions of the standard approach, I believe, demonstrate the twenty-one tacit lessons above. (p. 153)

Moreover, tasks such as drawing lines, filling in blanks, and circling, in and of themselves, often appear to be troubling to first-graders, as many of the children appear to have difficulty attending to physical tasks. This in turn requires first-grade teachers to spend a great deal of time focusing and holding children's attention on the specific tasks to be performed. In many cases it becomes almost a conditioning process. Physical directives ("Fold your hands") are often used by teachers to focus children's attention on specific tasks.

Teachers seem to rely heavily on physical tasks and frequently label them as providing "structure." One first-grade teacher remarked to me, after she had just finished defining and delineating a particular task to a group of students, "I'm sure you know that children need a lot of structure. You need to make this all a daily routine so that it becomes second nature to kids." Another teacher advised, "Even if you decide to use whole language with children, they are still going to need the structure they are used to getting. They deserve it and need it

---

* Reprinted with permission of Nancie Atwell: *In the Middle* (Boynton-Cook Publishers, Inc., Portsmouth, NH, 1987).

to succeed." The following reading lesson, which I observed, readily illustrates the degree of structure present in this first grade classroom.

Lesson 1

Teacher. Fold your hands. (She waits for quiet.) Now open your workbooks to page 20. Today we are going to do at least one page. Put your name on the top in D'Nealian (the script required by the district). Fold your hands. (The children go over letter sounds with their hands folded.)

Teacher. (Looking away from the reading group to the rest of the class.) Joshua has a warning! If it will help you be quiet, you can push your chair away from Trevor.

Teacher. (Attention is focused back to reading group.) Say the letters in the first box. Tommy, which letter does *fan* start with?

Tommy. (Pause) *f*.

Teacher. Good. Circle it.

Teacher. Bobby, what letter does *balloon* start with?

Bobby. (Pause) *b*.

Teacher. Good. Circle it. (The class does the first six examples together.)

Teacher. Now do the last six questions by yourself. Work carefully.

Carrie. (Confused) How do we do them?

Teacher. (Patiently) The same way we did the ones we did together. (The child nods and completes the entire page.)

Teacher. Is everyone finished?

Group. Yes.

Teacher. Good. We will correct that page tomorrow.

Teacher. Turn to the next page. We have to do the same thing on this page, but this time we have to write the correct letter on the line. (One of the children begins to tear out the page.) Don't be busy tearing the page out of your workbook instead of working. I will tell you when to tear out pages.

Teacher. Look at the first one. I will show you how to form the letter *b* properly in your workbook. (The teacher stands up and goes to the blackboard.) Try to get the middle of the *b* on the dotted line. Now, watch how we make a D'Nealian *f*. It is two spaces high. (She shows the group how to make the appropriate letters on the blackboard.)

Teacher. (Looking at the child's work.) You are making your *f*'s backwards.

Carrie. (Pointing at the *f*.) Whoops! (Child corrects all of her mistakes.)

Teacher. (Several seconds later) Good. Now those are *f*'s.

Teacher. (She continues to show the children how to make all the letters necessary to complete the page.) Now when we get to do these letters in handwriting, you will have a head start.

Teacher. (Speaking to one child) Why did you make your *s* one whole space high? Erase that and make a lower case *s*.

Sandy. (Puzzled) O.K.

Teacher. (Whispering) Run your thumb down the dotted line. Put your finger on one side of the binding. Tear out the page and close your book. Take your paper and put it in your mailbox and put your workbooks back on the desk without making any noise. (All of the children tiptoe back to their seats.)

The following is another example of a lesson from a first-grade classroom that is also characterized by structure and control.

Lesson 2

Teacher. "Carebears," please come up for reading. (Looking at me, she whispers) I like to call them second. They are really low, and have trouble concentrating. That's why I call them up when the room is really quiet.

Teacher. Francis, what are the names of these letters? (She holds flash cards up one at a time.)

Francis. (Tries to say them as quickly as possible) *s-l-m-t-r.*

Teacher. You got them all right except for this one. (She holds up the *p.*) This is a *p.* Remember? (Enthusiastically) You are doing much better. Boy, have you studied! You are on your way to more stickers!

Teacher. Everyone look at page 6 in your workbooks. (Pauses) Put your finger under the ant in the row. What letter does *ant* start with?

Group. (Pause) *a.*

Teacher. Good. Now circle the letter *a* in the first row. Now on the rest of the page, whenever you see an *a*, draw a line under it.

Teacher. No, Larry. You don't circle everything. You put a line under it.

Larry. (Confused) I don't know where to put the line.

Teacher. (Holding Larry's pencil) Under it, means right here.

Teacher. Put your finger under the first word in the next sentence. (The teacher puts Larry's finger in the proper place.)

Teacher. Every word in the sentence has a small *a.* Circle it.

Teacher. (Many children become confused.) Slow down.

Katie. I don't know which ones to circle, and which ones to underline.

Teacher. (Pauses) Let's do the rest of the page together. (She points to the letters that need to be circled. She repeats this with the letters to be underlined.)

Teacher. (The page is completed.) Any questions? That was hard! You have done a great job! Now, tiptoe back to your seats.

Teacher. Where does your paper belong when you get back to your seats?

Group: (They begin to stand up to go back to their seats.) In the top, right-hand corner.

Teacher. Good. That keeps things straight on the desks and helps you keep organized. (She then calls the next reading group.)

"Read the sentence and circle the picture," "Put a line under it," "Pick up your pencils," "Put them down, and fold your hands." This combination of structure, control, and physical task is typical, in varying degrees, of the classrooms observed in this study. It is little wonder that children's perceptions of reading are colored with statements such as, "Reading is when the teacher says circle the word, or you have to put a check on it." This type of teaching behavior was clearly in evidence and, in fact, dominated most of the reading lessons I observed. There seemed to be little opportunity for reading for meaning or pleasure in this setting.

In fact, pencil-and-paper tasks are frequently linked to physical tasks in both the minds of children and in the actual classroom setting. As previously discussed, teachers seem to use physical tasks to help focus first-graders on pencil-and-paper and other reading tasks. The following example illustrates the link between pencil-and-paper tasks and reading.

Teacher. (Class is standing, looking at a ditto on their desks.) Please read the words.

Class: (Words are read in unison.) *Flower, dig, hole, plant, seed,...*

Teacher. We are doing this to be certain you will be able to read the words independently.

Teacher. (Holds up ditto sheet) When you find an answer, should you draw a line through it?

Class: (In unison) No, we circle it.

Teacher. Mindy, please read the first sentence.

Mindy: (Reads aloud) "The flower was a seed at one time."

Teacher. Good! Mindy earned the right to sit down because she read the first sentence.

Teacher. (Walks to the blackboard and points to the date.) What else could you write on your paper besides, "It is Tuesday, February 16"?

Kevin: How about, "Mrs. Michel is visiting our class"?

Teacher: Great sentence! (The teacher has the student spell each word as she writes the sentence as a language experience story in front of the class.) Please read this together.

Class: (In unison) It is Tuesday, February... (As the children read correctly, she tells individuals they have "earned the right to sit down.")

At first glance, adults might think children are confused when they make responses such as "Reading is stand up, and sit back down." On the contrary, their perceptions reflect quite accurately the physical tasks in which they engage during instruction.

In addition to standing up and sitting down, first-graders are asked to "Walk quietly back and forth from your seats to reading group," "Color within the lines," "Stack papers in 'To Do' and 'Done' piles," "Fold your hands," "Sit up straight," and "Slide your fingers along under the words you are reading." Many of these physical tasks are reflected in the perceptions of the children interviewed in this study. Physical activity, when linked with instruction, clearly takes on reading-related meaning in the minds of first-graders.

HOME–SCHOOL DICHOTOMY

Children's perceptions are not tied exclusively to schools and classrooms. That is, children read books at home, they experience reading as they watch "Sesame Street" on television, they encounter print on their cereal boxes during breakfast, and even read street signs and billboards with their parents on their way to the babysitter's. Many first-graders had perceptions that evidenced a strong home influence. Most children also distinguished between reading in school and reading at home. They often engaged in a discussion of the differences between reading at home and reading at school. First-graders frequently stated that reading at home was "easier" than reading at school. As Jeffrey stated simply, "I can read at home best but I can't at school." Many of the comments were related to the various reading tasks performed in each setting, such as, "Reading at home is just reading books, and at school it's learning new words and papers."

Jeremy, a 6-year-old first-grader, enjoyed reading at home. One day, when I was helping Jeremy with his reading seatwork, he turned to me and said, unprompted:

We have to do too much seatwork at school. I'd rather read all the books in the world than do seatwork. Seatwork is the dumbest thing on earth.

I'd get to read more and be better at reading if she just gave us books instead of seatwork.

Jeremy was not the only first-grader to criticize seatwork. Ann very seriously explained:

Seatwork really is a waste of time, 'cuz nobody helps you with it, and if you do it really good you don't need to practice. I can see if it is something like 2 + 2 because you have to know it without counting on your fingers. But, we get so many papers to do every day. I rush to get them done. My teacher thinks I'm careless.

Ann further stated:

I am not careless when I do work at home. If I write a letter to my Grammy I want it to be really good. Sometimes, I do two copies, just to be sure it's right. I'm not careless when I read at home either, 'cuz I don't have to rush to get finished.

Other children further reflect on the content differences between the two. As Joshua remarked:

Books at school have only one sentence and then a period, and reading at home goes on and tells a story, and they have periods after lots of sentences on a page. I like the stories I read at home because I like to feel happy or sad because of a story. I feel kind of good when I'm reading a happy story and sad when it's a sad story. Stories make me feel things.

Max wistfully commented, "I thought in first grade we would get to read books. We do sometimes. But they are only reading books that have sentences on two pages. I like my books at home." Erin reflected on content differences and says, "In reading at school I play Bingo, do worksheets and workbooks and get seatwork and stuff, and at home I just read a book. That's more fun." Paul agreed that reading at home is more fun:

It's fun to read books at home. They are like the books in the library. Like Clifford is more fun than the stories in our school books. The story is much longer, so more things can happen. That makes the books more interesting.

It is noteworthy that when children discussed reading at school, they connected it only to what is done during reading group time. The seatwork was associated with reading because it was completed during the time other groups were being called to meet with the teacher. The reading-related activities done throughout the day were not associated in the minds of first-graders with reading at school. First-graders made it very clear that it was difficult to discuss reading without distinguishing between reading at home and reading at school.

It is also interesting that the children did not simply delineate the differences between reading at home and at school. Their comments were often evaluative in nature. They had definite opinions about these differences. Bradley felt, "Reading is when everyone gets to read. I read at school and not at home. So, I like reading at school. Nobody reads at home." Eric was even more definite:

> *I don't like reading at home because my mom makes me read to her. She never reads to me any more. She wants me to get better at reading. I like reading at school, because sometimes when the teacher calls us for reading, she reads to us instead.*

Stephen agreed as he commented, "Reading is special to me at school 'cuz nobody reads to me at my house." The reverse was true for Tiffany:

> *I like reading at home 'cuz me and my sister have a lot of books to read. Those books are lots better than reading books because they have more words in them and nice pictures and they're more interesting, too.*

Melissa talked about the dichotomy as truly puzzling when she commented:

> *Reading in school is writing in your books, but at home it's not writing in your books. Also, reading in school you tear out the pages in the book, but if you tear out the pages in the books at home you'd get in trouble and you wouldn't understand the story.*

As the above quotes illustrate, first-graders often naturally impose a dichotomy between reading at home and reading at school when they talk about reading. That is, reading at home and reading at school take on different meanings for first-graders. These perceptions generally center around the differences between the two in tasks performed. Most students who had very little exposure to reading at home showed that reading in school took on special meaning for them. For example, they talked about their teachers reading stories to them during reading time. Other children compared the content of basal readers, workbooks, and seatwork to trade books and stories, declaring the latter more interesting.

These first-graders certainly had definite opinions about the quality of reading at home and at school and readily alluded to the differences between the two. It would seem that both parents and teachers need to become more aware of the reading tasks in which they involve children and the profound influences these tasks have on children's perceptions.

The direct linkage between tasks and children's perceptions of reading has strong implications for both teachers and parents. Perhaps the most important lesson here is that children can be and often are "misled" about reading by the very tasks often used to teach reading. That is, the instructional tasks used in school may "mislead" first graders into thinking that reading is something other than a meaning-oriented process. Virtually every action taken in the name of reading results in a perceptual reaction on the part of the child, which shapes his or her schema of reading. Unfortunately, it appears that certain physical tasks, such as crossing out, underlining, and even standing up and sitting down, heavily dominate first-graders' perceptions of reading.

This study found that the reading tasks children are involved in at school significantly shape their perceptions of reading. Lindfors (1984) and Swanson (1985) have also suggested that the perceptions of reading and writing that children construct are closely tied to their reading and writing instructional experiences. Swanson notes:

> What cannot be discounted, however, is the impact of the reading program, per se, on the students' perceptions. The methodology and amount of instructional emphasis on various facets of the program will influence or formulate perceptions toward the learning to read process. (p. 128)

It is important that educators recognize that many children come to school with perceptions of reading congruent with the desired educational outcome, assuming that educators want children to equate reading with meaning. This study suggests that the "confusion" children exhibit is an outgrowth of the instruction they have received at school. When tasks such as "Stand up/sit down" or "Circle and underline the word" become part and parcel of reading instruction, children's perceptions of reading are colored by or even formed by those tasks. From the perspective of an adult, these perceptions can be misconstrued as confused or immature, when actually they are very logical conclusions drawn from circumstances in which children find themselves.

Interestingly, this study further indicates that children's perceptions are colored by instructional tasks regardless of methods and materials, and it further documents the influence of instruction on perceptions. First-graders' perceptions in all three of the settings observed were greatly influenced by the particular types of instruction they received. Children in the most "holistic" classroom defined reading initially as "the teacher writing down what you say on big paper" or "singing songs that have new words in them." It seems that regardless of methodology, curricula, or teacher philosophy, children's perceptions of reading mirror reading instruction.

The teachers who participated in this research were asked to read and respond to the "Results" section of this study and were notably surprised by their students' perceptions of reading. They were concerned when they found out that many of the day-to-day instructional tasks such as "Circle this" or "Color that" had taken on a disproportionate importance that was inconsistent with their instructional goals. Teachers often had a main objective for reading instruction (e.g., reading for meaning), which they facilitated by many subordinate activities (e.g., underlining words, circling letters). These subordinate activities often became the focus of day-to-day reading instruction and, therefore, dramatically influenced the children's understanding of what was most important.

The teachers found the descriptions of the children's perceptions compelling and, as a result, indicated that they intended to modify instruction to realign children's perceptions with the goals of their reading programs. The teachers felt that their focus and actual instructional practices must be changed from physical reading-related tasks to reading for meaning. This is evidence of what teachers can learn from their students and emphasizes the crucial role that listening to children can play in providing appropriate instruction.

Because many first-graders said worksheets were often a "waste of time," teachers might look at each and every one of those worksheets and ask if it can be justified. Although it is true that children don't always know what is best for them or may not fully understand the purpose or value of an activity a teacher chooses, it is equally true that their input can help a busy teacher to pause and reflect on whether certain activities are really the best way to accomplish an objective or reach a goal. Teachers might also examine what percentage of each week is spent on meaning-oriented reading for each instructional reading group. If teachers are serious about increasing "real" reading, as opposed to isolated drill on the parts, they will have to be more selective in the use of skills sheets. Educators cannot expect their first-grade students to view reading as "a search for meaning" when so much instructional time is spent pursuing tasks that, when viewed from a child's perspective, are not at all connected to reading for meaning.

It has been shown that instruction can sometimes fail because students interpret instruction differently from what teachers intend. For example, beginning readers are often urged to sound out unknown words. They frequently make sounds and blend them together but do not associate any meaning with the sounds. The teacher might assume that the child has identified a meaningful word, when in reality the child has identified nothing more than the component sounds of a word. Student learning is clearly enhanced when students perceive the intent of teachers' instruction (Winne & Marx, 1982). The first-graders I studied certainly confirmed this.

By asking and listening to what children think about reading, and using children's perceptions as one gauge for instructional effectiveness, teachers can better facilitate continuing growth as they build on what children already know. In addition, parents would do well to resist the temptation of duplicating nonmeaningful, task-oriented, pedantic classroom practices at home and continue to make reading as meaningful and pleasurable as possible. It is easy for parents to be tempted by all the workbooks that are readily available today, even in neighborhood grocery stores. However, time can be better spent by simply reading stories with their children.

A Classroom Teacher Responds...

We spend 180 days a year with a classroom full of children who are ready to learn and eager to succeed. Yet we, as teachers, seem to be unaware of these children's views on something as significant as reading. This chapter challenges me to walk back into my classroom tomorrow and begin to listen, observe, and dialogue more carefully with my students regarding their reading activities.

Many upper grades today are using more self-evaluation tools. Why not ask younger children to respond orally to a reading theme, a unit of study, or a daily lesson? Listen to their feedback. What did they learn? Did they already know this information? What would they like to read? What reading activities would they enjoy? They have so much to tell us that we can learn in no other way!

Certainly, children need to know letters, sounds, and vocabulary, but the learning process can be much more exciting and meaningful than daily doses of ditto and workbook skill pages. For example, why not find a story with lots of *b* words, read the story, and then scrutinize the pages in search of *big, beautiful B* words?

Why not find a story with a repetitive pattern, read it, read it again as a choral activity, and then find the words that were used repeatedly. You could then together develop a sight word list from the stories read, rather than learning words from an isolated list provided by an outside source.

I was surprised that this study found similar perceptions of reading by children in traditional and more holistic classrooms. It really struck a nerve when I read that some children viewed reading as "singing songs with new words in them." "That's fine by me," was my initial reaction. But I now realize that using a song or a poem or a story to teach a skill or a vocabulary word is still a method. Even with a song, I will now remember to sing it as a whole, enjoy it, and respond to it from my own point of view and prior knowledge. Then I can involve children in activities such as searching for words (e.g., *see/ sea, mist/ missed*) that sound the same but are spelled differently in "Puff the Magic Dragon," or discussing the number of syllables in "Supercalifragilisticexpialidocious."

If reading for meaning is our goal, and I believe it is, we need to offer our students extended opportunities to enjoy real literature, as opposed to contrived or artificial stories written to teach a skill, and provide better and more natural ways to enhance the acquisition of necessary skills. Why can't we have children write and illustrate their own books daily? The books might be as simple as a few words per page (using invented spelling). These books would hold special meaning for the children. Along with a wide variety of trade books, the children's original stories could be displayed and read by all. Flexible reading groups could meet for specific instruction, for sharing ideas, or to share original works. The groups might be based on immediate individual needs, and therefore the composition would change often. Maybe then the children would be less apt to see reading as isolated tasks such as circling, underlining, and crossing out.

Parents Respond...

It seems to us, based on our own children's reading, that learning to read must involve several major elements:

- Motivation
- Process
- Assessment and adjustment
- Reinforcement/affirmation

It seems that children will be motivated if they find reading a pleasurable experience and/or see its relevance to their lives and if they believe they are making progress in mastering the process. It is clear from the quotations in this chapter that reading stories with children at home can go a long way toward their concluding that reading is pleasurable and, therefore, good. Thus, we parents can play a critical role in delivering to the schoolteacher a student who is eager to continue the learning-to-read process. We never realized before how vital our role as parents is in helping our children learn to read.

We can see now how teachers must wrestle with the question of how much structure is appropriate for individual students to master the learning-to-read process without bogging them down and losing motivation. How much "circling, underlining, and crossing out" is necessary? At least some worksheets seem to be viewed positively by some children. Sometimes, our own kids brought them home and bragged, "That was a cinch," or, "Look, I got these all right." Often we had the impression that our children considered particular worksheets to be a game or puzzle.

The author asserts that "reading for meaning" is the main objective of reading instruction and that day-to-day instructional activities such as circling, underlining, and crossing out take on disproportionate importance and often impede achievement of the main objective. This understanding is true from our point of view, as well, although clearly there have been time periods as our children learned to read during which word mechanics seemed to consume their attention. We have seen our children go through numerous learning stages. Our children all focused for a time on tackling words—not on reading comprehension. Teachers and parents should not be too concerned with this temporal focus on structure, unless the child stalls at this stage or becomes discouraged. Our son's perception of reading changed after a month of school as he began talking more about reading in terms of words and letters, but later he seemed to focus again on figuring out what the story meant.

This chapter shows that children's perceptions of reading at school and at home indeed can differ. Our goal as parents and teachers should be to make both perceptions positive. Just as teachers can create a negative perception by overemphasizing reading mechanics and structure, so parents can fail to foster positive perceptions. For example, in many homes, parents read little or not at all with their children. At the other extreme, some parents buy workbooks at the grocery store to give their children added practice, thereby giving skills more importance than reading for pleasure. It appears that teachers cannot count on positive perceptions emanating from the home. This must make the teacher's job doubly difficult.

We again conclude that continual parent–teacher–child communication is important. Teachers need to know what perceptions of reading children bring to school from their home environment, parents need to know children's perceptions of how the instructional process is working at school, and teachers and parents need to communicate as much as possible to ensure that their efforts are consistent in helping children see reading as a meaningful process.

▶ 4

Processing Print: More Than Just Sounds

PREVIEW

This chapter will give you insights into how first-graders actually process print. You will see that children are able to understand and describe the reading process. "Sounding out" was most frequently mentioned by children in this study as the approach they used when reading unknown words; however, first-graders' understandings of the reading process are not limited to decoding or sounding out words. They demonstrate a meaning-oriented understanding of reading, as well.

This chapter illustrates that first-graders have a rich understanding of the reading process. Like Chapter 2, it will demonstrate how classroom practices influence children's perceptions. After reading this chapter, you will also see how important meaningful reading is to early reading acquisition. The richness of the children's perceptions shared in this chapter may encourage you to listen carefully to your students as you examine your own teaching.

MR. FRANK'S READING GROUP

The children were sprawled on the reading rug. Mr. Frank sat among them and encouraged each one to take a turn reading aloud. The majority of the group pointed as they read, in turn, *Arthur's Honeybear,* by Lillian Hoban. When Paula's turn came, she read with confidence and certainty. Although she miscalled words on occasion, the words she substituted made sense in the context of the story. Mr. Frank permitted Paula to read on and did not seem concerned when she misread the words. Paula hesitated when she came to two unfamiliar words. The first word, climb, was supplied immediately by Mr. Frank. On the second word, *desk,* Mr. Frank supplied only the initial consonant sound and asked Paula to sound it out. Paula put her finger under *esk,* moved her lips, looked at Mr. Frank, and said, "Desk."

Blair read next, with a great deal less certainty. He used his finger as he laboriously read the text, word byword and sometimes letter by letter. The other children in the group seemed to grow impatient with Blair's approach. But Mr. Parks remained patient and supplied numerous words for Blair. He permitted Blair to sound out many of the words and frequently encouraged him with prompts such as, "Sound out the first part," "First letter is *p,*" and "Sound *pot.*"

Marsha, meanwhile, pointed and moved her finger under each word and subvocalized whenever Blair and Mr. Frank sounded out words together. When it was her turn to read, her finger moved slightly behind the words she was actually decoding. When she attempted to sound out words, it was clear that she had little knowledge in this area. Her major word attack strategy seemed to be guessing from the context and/or attempting to remember the configuration of words on sight. Even though Marsha lacked the skill to decode words systematically, Mr. Frank encouraged her to "sound it out" time after time. More often than not, Mr. Frank resorted to saying the word segments for her, and Marsha would then blend the sounds together in an attempt to pronounce the word. Often the words she produced in this manner were pronounced like nonwords. That is, even for what sounded like a word, there was no recognition in Marsha's voice as she blended the sounds together. She was sounding out words in a vacuum, attaching no meaning to them.

The reading group time concluded with a discussion of the story the participants had read. Mr. Frank questioned the children about their reading and helped them relate the story to their everyday lives. He showed great concern that each child in the group understood what they had read. The children enthusiastically discussed the story and often interjected anecdotes of their own. Mr. Frank was quick to refocus the group back to the story, in a kind way, and seemed concerned that the group "move along." The lesson ended with Mr. Frank assigning a new story to be read silently at the children's seats.

CHILDREN'S PERCEPTIONS: PROCESS

It is clear that the children in Mr. Frank's group made use of a number of reading strategies necessary to "unlock" both the word and meaning codes of the story. In addition to describing reading tasks, these same first-graders also evidenced a deep understanding of the processes they employ when learning to read and/or actually reading. That is, they were able to discuss specific physical and/or cognitive strategies they utilized when they encountered print. Often, their discussion of the reading processes they employed centered around what they did when they encountered unknown words. Perhaps not surprisingly, decoding unknown words appeared to be a major issue for first-graders and significantly influenced how they thought about reading.

Sounding out words was by far the most frequently mentioned approach utilized to "unlock" the unknown words. Some, like Douglas, mentioned two strategies employed for attacking new words. "Reading is a lot of words. Some are hard and some are easy. An easy word you just say and a hard word you sound out." Others spoke only of sounding words out; Rebecca said, "I'm learning to read. If you don't know some of the words, you can sound them out. I like sounding out short words." Other first-graders, like Melissa, were able to activate the actual cognitive processes employed in decoding unknown words. She clearly demonstrated an understanding that words are composed of letters which when put together or blended form a "stretched out word." "Reading is words made from letters. You put letters together to make words.

You need to put the letters together to stretch words out." Melissa's notion of stretched-out words seems to correspond with the long, drawn-out phonemic word method (e.g., *b-l-a-c-k*), modeled by teachers and then produced by students in the instructional setting.

Not all children employed sounding out as a reading strategy. Some, like Joanna, though aware of sounding out as a strategy, chose not to utilize it. "I already know the words by looking at them so I don't have to sound them out." Joanna's comment suggests not only an awareness of sounding out as a strategy, but an understanding of when to activate it as well. Her remark could be interpreted in terms of an understanding of how some words are recognized at sight and the inappropriateness of attempting to sound out words that are already part of a sight word vocabulary. Beth seemed to have a more involved perception of the reading process, which goes beyond simply sounding out unknown words or recognizing others by sight:

> *I think I sort of have to sound the words out if I forget to read the words. I'm reading the sentence in my head without looking at the pictures. I'm hearing the words, not seeing the pictures. My Mom and Dad tell me about when they were little and think of what it's like if I go back there. When I read a book I do the same thing and imagine it is really happening.*

Here we have Beth seemingly contemplating what she is reading, as a word recognition strategy. Yet phrases like, "think of what it's like if I go back there" and "imagine it is really happening" suggest that she is attempting to connect meaning with the sound-it-out strategy she comments on initially in her quote. It is interesting to note that she felt it necessary to qualify her comment about sounding out words she has forgotten with a statement about pictures. Beth replied, "I'm reading the sentence in my head without looking at the pictures" and "I'm hearing the words, not seeing the pictures." Her statements suggest an awareness that pictures can be used to help identify words and that, without their help, she must rely more on actually sounding out the word. One also gets the feeling that perhaps Beth has been made to feel that looking at the pictures is in some way cheating, as she was almost reassuring me as she spoke that she was processing without the pictures. She also demonstrated a strong under-standing of visualizing or creating a picture in her mind as another reading strategy. Her allusion to her Mom and Dad's remembrance of "what it's like" "back there" further suggests an awareness of visualizing an image as a useful strategy.

Not all children are as comfortable with sounding out as Rebecca and Beth. The physical act of "sounding out" words silently was difficult for Mindy. "Our teacher makes us read quietly. No matter how hard I try, I have to move my lips when I read and the words just come out." Eddie was unable to identify the component sounds of words and therefore found sounding it out very difficult:

The teacher tells me to sound it out, but sometimes I don't know what sounds the letters make or I forget. So, when I sound it out it don't sound right. So she says the sounds, then I say the sounds, then I get it.

Still others, like Frankie, seemed to have difficulty putting the sounds together to make words:

When I sound it out sometimes I can't hear it. I say it, but I can't hear it. When my teacher says it, I hear it, and then I say it and read it. But when I say it, it's hard to hear.

First-graders are very resourceful and have found numerous ways of circumventing the obstacles often encountered when sounding out words. One of the most frequently employed strategies is simply to seek help with unknown words. Tim used a combination of asking his brother and sounding out as a strategy. "A lot of times I don't try to sound out the words before I ask my brother. I only sound them out if he's not home." Parents also come to the rescue of beginning readers:

First, I look at the word and if I don't know it my Mommy helps me. I don't know how to sound the words out but I look at the whole word and try it. Then I ask my Mommy.

Some children have heard their teachers say, "Sound the word out," but have little understanding of what this actually means. Kristen said:

I am reading because the teacher tells me to sound words out. First I look at the word and if I don't know my Mommy helps me. My teacher thinks I know how to sound the words out, but I don't know what that means. I look at the whole word and try it. Then I ask Mommy or a friend.

Kevin was also struggling with the concept of sounding words out:

I have three books at home that I can read. You learn to read by sounding words out. I'm not sure what that means, so when the teacher says to sound the word out I look at the whole word.

Heather also had little understanding of the phrase "sound it out":

My teacher always tells me to sound it out, but I don't know what that means. I just move my finger and my lips cuz she does. Please don't tell her. I should have learned that in kindergarten. I don't think any of the kids in Carebears can sound the words out either.

Children who have no understanding of "sound it out" clearly are at a disadvantage when placed in instructional settings that require that this strategy be employed. Teachers who teach sounding out as a decoding strategy should be certain that their students understand what the concept means before assuming they can use it or asking them to use it to unlock unknown words. The words themselves present sufficient problems, which when compounded with a lack of understanding of the concept "sound it out," would seem to be almost insurmountable to a beginning reader.

One way to know if students understand a particular concept is to come right out and ask them in a nonthreatening way, and then truly listen to them as they respond. Children know when questions are being asked because the teacher really wants to know an answer in order to understand the child better or in order to make instructional decisions. They learn quickly when questions are being asked simply because they are contained in a teacher's manual or an interview questionnaire. John Holt, in *Learning All the Time* (1989), demonstrates the importance of listening to children and shows great respect for their knowledge and perceptions. He offers this about listening to children:

> One of the things you find in listening to the conversations of children is that the questions that little kids ask themselves about the world are likely to be very big questions, not little ones. They don't ask, "Why does the water come out of the tap?" Instead they ask, "Where did the universe come from?" (p. 156)

Children don't always ask the questions or give the responses that we expect. We have to be ready for the surprises and value what is important to them.

First-graders' understandings of the reading process are not always limited to decoding or sounding out unknown words. Most demonstrated an understanding of reading as a meaning-oriented process, as well. As Michael explained:

> *Reading means making sense out of reading books or take home books. The letters are important for sounding words out, but the words mean something. I can read words, sentences, and books. Reading is to help you understand things.*

Tanya said, "I think reading helps you understand things. You read to understand a story." Jennifer not only acknowledged that meaning exists, but she put meaning ahead of word recognition in importance; Jennifer was one first-grader who wasn't about to get bogged down by the unknown words in the story. "It doesn't matter if you can read every word as long as you know what the story is about. That's the most important part of reading." Krystal had a meaning-oriented vision of reading when she commented, "Reading is reading a book. It is understanding what the story means. How would you know if you like a book or hate a book if you don't know what it means?" Tim, on the other hand, demonstrated an understanding of the importance of decoding to the overall understanding of a story. His comments, though comprehension-oriented, evidenced an understanding of how the whole story is influenced by the contributing parts. "If I read the word but don't know what it says, sometimes I go ask somebody so I can go on with the story, so I'll understand the story." Melissa was more of a pragmatist in her understanding and acknowledgment of the importance of comprehension. "The words in the story have to make sense. If *s-t-o-p* didn't mean *stop*, you wouldn't know when to stop. Everyone would crash." Curtis also focused on meaning:

> *If you have a book in front of you, you read it and try to understand what it means so you can learn. You read instructions so you can understand them and do good work. One time I didn't think about what the directions meant, so I got 'em all wrong. The words tell you what it's about when you read.*

Beth showed a real emphasis on reading for meaning as she enthusiastically said, "When I read I imagine it is really happening." Once again we see visualization being employed as a strategy, but here as an assist to comprehension instead of an assist to decoding. Rebecca focused on meaning through the use of pictures and text as she stated, "Reading is reading words and it tells you about the pictures. Pictures help me understand what the story is about." Hillary continued to focus on reading for meaning, although she found that some reading tasks don't make sense. "Reading is doing papers and when we get to read sentences, they sometimes tell us a story. Sometimes the papers at seatwork time don't make sense. But the stories do."

As these quotations illustrate, first-graders have a real understanding of the reading processes they employ when reading. Children frequently alluded to "sounding out words" and asking friends and/or family for help when needed. These same children not only included the "word attack" strategies described here as part of the reading process, but evidenced a deep sense of reading for meaning as well.

PROCESS: HOW IT COMES TO BE

In the act of reading, readers must "process" print in some way. This print is internalized by readers, as indicated by the foregoing quotations, to arrive at meaning. Children are taught to process print in a variety of ways. The processes employed in school do, of course, have an impact on children's perceptions of reading. Most common is the perception that reading has something to do with "sounding out words."

This finding became clearer as I examined the different types of activities that were observed in all three instructional settings. When children were in reading group, they were participating in one or more of a number of possible activities. These activities include:

1. Orally dictating a story to be written by the teacher or reading a story from a basal reader or a trade book ("round robin" or as a whole group)
2. Answering questions pertaining to that story
3. Participating in a reading skills lesson (participation includes either listening to the teacher talk about a skill or practicing the skill) utilizing the actual context of the story, workbook pages, or ditto sheets
4. Listening to directions explaining independent seatwork to be completed after reading group instruction
5. Correcting workbooks or worksheets

Each of the above activities usually involved some form of workbook, worksheet activity, and/or word analysis instruction.

In *Broken Promises,* Patrick Shannon (1989) describes reading group time in a similar way. He concludes that students are doing one of the following seven activities:

1. Listening to or reading a story from a basal anthology
2. Answering questions about that story
3. Listening to teachers present information about a reading skill
4. Practicing that skill with the teacher
5. Completing a criterion-referenced test
6. Listening to directions on how to complete assignments to be finished during seatwork
7. Correcting worksheets or workbooks

He further concludes that "Seatwork occupies twice as much student time as the group lessons, and typically workbooks and worksheets are predominant during this independent activity" (p. 95). I observed that "sounding out" was the dominant strategy taught to beginning readers by their teachers when children encounter words they can not read at sight, regardless of the instructional setting. A great deal of the first-grade instruction was directed at mastering phonics, and children spent a great deal of time talking about the "sounds made by letters." Children sang songs about letters, matched letter sounds with pictures in workbooks, and cut out pictures to go with sounds like muh, puh, and kuh. Most first-graders learn that "*A* is for *apple.*" Indeed, sound–symbol correspondence instruction was a major component of much of the reading instruction delivered by first-grade teachers. Children were frequently observed pointing to word parts and softly voicing the sounds made by those portions of the words. Fingers were frequently moved through words from left to right. First-graders were also observed covering up parts of words as they sounded them out. Teachers seemed to encourage this physical assistance and frequently modeled these behaviors for the children.

Even peers got into the sound-it-out instructional act. In one room I visited, the children were reading orally in reading group when one child encountered an unknown word. Another child in the group attempted to help by whispering, "It starts with muh." The teacher added, "It rhymes with *take*." The child was encouraged by another reading group member to "sound it out"; thus *make* became *make*, and everyone was happy. First-grade teachers frequently instructed their children, "If you don't know a word, look at the beginning and ending sounds."

Teachers taught their students other strategies as well. They demonstrated how pictures could be used to figure out unknown words, showed how and when to "guess" at a word, and gave examples of when sounding out wasn't appropriate. As one teacher instructed, "Some words just can't be sounded out. You just have to know them." It is little wonder that children's perceptions of reading contain phrases like these:

"I already knew the word by looking at it, so I didn't have to sound it out."

"If you know some of the words, you can sound out words you don't know."

"I like sounding out short words."

The ultimate strategy, offered by one very practical first-grader, was, "First I look at the word, and if I don't know it, I ask my Mommy." Children have internalized an understanding of many of the processes they utilize when learning to decode words. This understanding is rich, indeed, and is shaped by instructional practices.

Although "sounding out" dominates first-grade reading instruction, first-graders' understanding of the reading process goes beyond decoding known and unknown words. These same first-graders' perceptions also suggest that they have a real sense of the comprehension process. Most of the children, regardless of their instructional context, commented about words in stories having to "make sense," "being able to answer questions about a story," "feeling happy or sad after reading a story" or "thinking about what stories are about."

Once again, an examination of classroom reading instruction will give us a better understanding of the nature of the first-graders' perceptions. Children are asked to read sentences and match them with appropriate pictures, draw pictures to go with stories, and put sentences in sequential order to make a story. They are asked questions about what they have read and are encouraged to "think" about what they have just read. They are given purpose-setting questions such as, "Read the first page silently and think about the answers to these two questions: 'What did the girl find in the workshop?' and 'What did the girl want to make?' " This sort of instruction focuses children's attention on the reading comprehension process, and that focus seems to be reflected in children's perceptions of reading, as well. As these examples illustrate, students' perceptions of reading processes appear to be linked with the types of experiences these children have with reading at school.

First-graders are typically taught to "process" print in many ways, and those processes become part of their understanding of what reading is all about. Children are not mistaken when they suggest that "reading is letters" or "reading is sounding words out." Again, they are accurately reflecting common instructional practices.

The first-graders in this study had perceptions that were heavily dominated by a phonic interpretation of the reading process. That is, they talked a great deal about "sounding words out" and "what you do when you only know the first sound"; and they defined reading as the sounds of the letters. They appeared to have a clear understanding of many of the strategies they had been taught in reading, and these strategies had become part of their definition.

It is important to note, however, that although these children understood that "sound it out" was part of what reading is all about, by their own admission many did not understand what "sound it out" actually meant. This situation can be problematic. If a teacher prompts children to sound out unknown words, and children respond by physically moving their finger from left to right under a word, while moving their lips and uttering inaudible sounds, reading acquisition is not enhanced. Children are merely responding to the sound-it-out directive with a behavior that will satisfy the teacher's expectation. Fortunately, this study identifies the fact that children know when they don't understand what "sound it out" means and can articulate their uncertainty when asked. However, the teacher must be sensitive to the fact that many first-graders have spent a great deal of energy trying to figure out what this concept means, with little or no success. Therefore, some children may fear being found out and may not admit to this lack of understanding too readily.

Asking students what they understood about what was said, checking for individual differences in interpretation, inquiring about the cues that students used to determine teacher intent, and assessing a student's perceptions are all important strategies that teachers might use to help evaluate their own instruction and prevent misunderstandings in communication with their students. Specific questions ("Christopher, when I say 'Sound a word out,' what do you do?") could be asked casually during noninstructional times. The tone will let the child know that the question is meant as a tool to guide teacher effectiveness, rather than a weapon. Pearson and Johnson (1978) advise that the issue "is not whether or not to use questions, but how, when and where they ought to be used" (p. 154).

In addition to "sound it out," numerous other strategies are taught to children in order to help them master the reading process. Teachers are encouraged to remember that the instructional processes they employ in the classroom seem to have a significant impact on children's perceptions of reading and that first-graders can tell us whether or not we are communicating clearly. Therefore, improving our listening skills, questioning skills, and data-gathering skills could be extremely helpful in modifying instruction in order to better meet the needs of our students.

The first-graders in this study not only included decoding as a part of the reading process, but discussed the importance of reading for meaning as well. Children did not use adult-constructed jargon such as "comprehension" but talked about "seeing pictures of the story in their minds," loving to read "because storybooks make you happy or sad depending on what they are about," or "imagining all the funny things that Clifford did." These types of statements all reflect a very deep sense of reading for meaning. When children talked about getting meaning from the printed page, they were less likely to discuss tasks or instructional strategies. Rather, they talked of personal reading experiences. It appears that most first-graders do not associate meaning with instruction. This is an area of concern for teachers if the major objective of reading instruction is to derive meaning from print. It is very clear, however, that children's understanding of the reading process was rich indeed and often included an understanding of reading for meaning.

These rich and full understandings did not surface in the initial interview situation. The children seemed to be attempting to give adult answers that they felt would satisfy adult questions about reading. The rich, meaning-oriented perceptions surfaced only when children felt comfortable and began talking spontaneously about what reading meant to them. Therefore, when examining children's perceptions of reading, educators must recognize that children's initial responses may be constructed to please the adult and may not represent all that the child actually knows.

When children say reading is "math," "taking out your books and pencils," "looking at stories on big paper," or "sounding out words," they are demonstrating an understanding of the form and content of classroom reading instruction. These comments do not suggest that first-graders are unaware of the importance of reading for meaning, nor do they reveal that the children are confused or mistaken. They do show, however, that first-graders think about the types of reading tasks and processes in which they participate at school and their perceptions of reading reflect that understanding.

A Classroom Teacher Responds...

The message, "Listen to children; they have much to offer" continues to intrigue me. I think of my own 6-year-old, who, when asked, "What did you do in school today?" always responds with a vague, superficial response. But when he is gently prodded or ready to talk, he describes tasks, his reactions, and the input of others in depth. It is true that children know and understand much more than we give them credit for. As adults we can pay attention to them; as teachers we must respond to their perceptions.

After I read this chapter, the implications for reading instruction became clear for me. When a child is struggling with a strategy like "Sound it out," "Use context," or "Look at the pictures," the teacher must be certain that the strategy is understood. What do those words mean to a child? A teacher might model the strategy for the child to provide a more useful approach at that time. The last thing I want to do is reinforce the belief that "I can't do it." When I tell a child to "sound it out," I can no longer assume that the child knows what I mean. This chapter has shown me the importance of listening to children in order to build effectively on what they know. Success breeds success, and my job is to provide the success.

I felt that many aspects of Mr. Frank's reading instruction were positive and instructionally sound. I was happy to find him in the midst of children on the reading rug. I nodded in agreement as he simply supplied a word for a child when she first hesitated and as he allowed another reader to continue reading when a word that made sense contextually was substituted. Mr. Frank was patient and encouraging as his students read. But by the time Mr. Frank's reading group ended, I was no longer as pleased. I wondered why, when the children were having trouble with a word and the sound-it-out approach was not working, he didn't ask them to read the words surrounding the unknown word and figure it out from context. Maybe we do just say things like "sound it out" automatically without even thinking.

Certainly each teacher has a favorite instructional strategy (and I guess mine is reading in context), but the best reading instruction responds to individual needs of the children. I was pleased to see that so many children had developed a deep sense of reading for meaning in this study. I was distressed, however, to see that this perception seems to be associated with places other than school. As teachers, we need to examine all types of strategies, prioritize their value for most children, and then individualize our approach for specific children.

Hurray for Jennifer in this chapter, who sums it up so well: "It doesn't matter if you can read every word as long as you know what the story is about." Perhaps that is the message we should be delivering to all students, at all grade levels, at all times!

Parents Respond...

Our experience with our three children confirms the author's conclusion that children employ a variety of tactics to "break" word and meaning codes of stories. If they do not recognize an entire word on sight, they tend to try "sounding out" first. If that technique is not successful, however, they fall back on a series of other methods. These techniques (not necessarily in the order attempted) include seeking clues from pictures on the page, considering the context in which the word is used, trying to associate the word with some other word already mastered (e.g., *bake* looks like *make*, but it starts with a *b*, and the *b* sound is *buh*, so the word must be *bake*), and asking for help. It seems reasonable on the basis of the children's comments that adults can assist kids greatly by making it clear to them that there are indeed a number of ways to "read" words and by encouraging them to try any and all approaches. We can impede children's progress if we lead them to believe there is only one approach, or just a few approaches, or one best approach. Children should come to understand that they have many strategies available to them and that it is fair to use them all.

In reading with our children as they have been struggling with beginning reading, we've always told them not to worry if they're slow in figuring out a word. Speed doesn't count. Furthermore, it's O.K. to make mistakes. It's trying that is important. Reading words is sometimes like solving a mystery or puzzle. You keep trying "clues" until you have a solution.

Our children, like most children these days, have been exposed to computers at school, beginning in kindergarten. There is a very popular children's software program that our children play at home and at school, called *Where in the World Is Carmen Sandiego?* In *Carmen*, kids use clues about various nations to find out where Carmen Sandiego and her gang of master thieves are hiding. Our younger children have played *Carmen* with their older siblings before they have learned to read. Explaining that reading words is like using clues in *Carmen* to solve a mystery has helped us eliminate our children's concerns about reading, make "unlocking" words a fun game, and help them learn to process print.

Purpose: Whose?

PREVIEW

This chapter will expose you to the wide range of purposes that first-graders have for reading. You will see how their experiences at home and at school lead to the development of rich and meaningful understandings of why they read. You will also see how systematic, direct reading instruction can lead to the development of limited motives for reading.

After reading this chapter you may be more reluctant to use the materials-driven, purpose-setting questions often found in published reading materials. Instead, you will be encouraged to spend time talking with your students to find out more about their personal reasons for reading and incorporate them into your reading instruction.

THE BABYSITTER

Karen stood on the curb holding Kevin's hand. As soon as the "WALK" sign appeared, Kevin yelled out in his best and proudest reading voice, "Walk!" He and Karen then marched across the street together. Karen had always wanted to be a teacher, so she was particularly thrilled to be babysitting the Johnsons' son.

Kevin, a first-grader, liked taking walks with Karen because she paid a great deal of attention to him. Every time they came to one of the familiar signs on the street, he happily announced, "Bakery," "Stop," "Exit," "Police Station," or anything else he happened to recognize on his way up the street. Kevin and Karen made trips to the library two or three times a week. Karen quickly learned that a trip to the library made the three-hour babysitting chore much more pleasant for both her and Kevin.

Once inside the library, Kevin knew to quiet down and use his "library voice." Today they chose two books to read together: *Best Friends*, by Steven Kellogg, and a *Time–Life* Book entitled *Wheels and Wings*. Kevin relaxed while Karen read the storybook to him. Occasionally he looked at the pictures, but for the most part he just listened as Karen read in her best "teacher voice."

When the book with the car on the cover came out, however, Kevin's attitude changed. He hovered over Karen's shoulder and pointed to various cars as he identified them by name. Kevin said, "My dad drives a four by four. He likes Chevys best. This one's a Chevy. I know the word Chevy. I know that word, too. It's 'tractor.' This one says 'tractor trailer.' You see, there's two words, and 'tractor trailer' has two parts."

Lately, Kevin had become very interested in learning new information from books. He had begun to select many nonfiction books to help him with projects. For example, Kevin urged, "Let's get the birdhouse book again and try to build another one." Karen quickly dismissed this idea, as they were almost out of time, and she did not want to pursue something of that magnitude again. On the way home, she distracted Kevin from the birdhouse idea and focused his attention on reading the signs once more.

As they got closer to home, Karen began quizzing Kevin about his homework. For the past several months, Karen had taken on another important responsibility with Kevin. He was beginning to bring assignments home from school—unlearned words, spelling, unfinished work—and she was instrumental in helping him with his tasks.

"What did you do in reading today, Kevin?"

Kevin answered, "Oh, we did some worksheets."

Karen then asked, "Did you finish them all?"

"Well, no," Kevin admitted. "I still have one to finish."

Karen inquired, "What do we have to do? What kind of work is it?"

Kevin answered, "I don't know. It may be a word hunt."

Karen reassured him, "Word hunts are easy. Don't worry about that. We can have it finished before I leave. Don't you have any questions to do?"

Kevin replied, "I have a story and questions, but Mom likes to help me with those. I can do the questions with her tonight."

Karen asked, "Is the teacher still upset at the way you do the questions, or did you have a chance to talk to her?"

Kevin replied, "No, I've figured out that the answers are right in the book, and you can make the answers right. I'm getting good at finding the answers in the stories. I just copy them right from the book. She likes that 'cuz I get them right and spell everything right."

Karen said, "That's great. When we get home we can do the word hunt, and then we can go outside and play for awhile."

This trip to the library clearly demonstrates the degree of exposure to print that this first-grader experiences daily. It also illustrates how Kevin encounters reading in a variety of settings, how reading in these settings takes on different meanings, and how one approaches reading differently in each of these situations. Reading has various purposes. Kevin read traffic signs, street signs, and billboards—all examples of environmental print that he encountered on the way to the library. He also experienced the recreational aspect of reading as he and Karen shared library books, just for fun. He read to learn new information as he became interested in knowing more about cars and building birdhouses. Finally, on his way home he was able to shift to thinking about an instructional setting and could articulate clearly to Karen what was required in his school reading. He knew that he must find the answer to the question and copy it down accurately with correct spelling.

CHILDREN'S PERCEPTIONS: REASONS FOR READING

In all cases, Kevin has demonstrated a clear understanding of a variety of purposes for reading. This research study of first-graders' perceptions demonstrates that these rich understandings of purposes for reading are not unique to Kevin. In fact, first-graders' perceptions of reading illustrate that they clearly have different purposes for reading and that they can explain why they are reading. It is evident that these purposes emerge from a variety of settings.

The responses from my interviews with first-graders clearly indicate that their understandings of what reading is all about include a recognition on their part of purposeful reading. That is, when asked about why they read, the children in this study were able to articulate well-thought-out reasons for reading and/or for learning to read.

By and large, their reasons for reading were personal in nature and, though meaningful, seldom were akin to the purpose-setting instruction that was an important feature of many of their reading programs and a frequently taught skill in their reading groups. The probable reason for this is that this purpose-setting component often had little to do with the children's lives or personal reasons for reading. When the children did link purposeful reading to instruction, they typically reduced purposes for reading to some type of school task to be performed in a certain way or completed in a specific time interval.

As John stated, "Reading is to keep us busy. I mostly like to go out and play, but most times I can't go out 'cuz my work isn't done." John's comment, with its tight connection to task completion and punitive measures, is clearly inconsistent with how most teachers would like to see first-graders think about reading. It also seems to place an unnecessary obstacle in the path to reading success for this first-grader. How is John to come to understand, learn from, and appreciate reading when he views it as busy-work and something to be done before he can go out and play?

Stephen's understanding of why he is learning to read was more closely related to the pragmatics of successfully negotiating his way through the pass/fail requirements of school. He simply and succinctly stated that the purpose of reading is "So you can pass first grade." Again, there was no mention of pleasure, information gathering, or learning that we would hope to hear a first-grade student connect with reasons for reading. His school reading agenda seems to focus on passing first grade.

Beth is another first-grader whose school-oriented understanding of reading lacked a personal component. She simply stated, "It's important to learn to read so you can do your reading seatwork." How could Beth have possibly come to this limited perception of why she is learning to read? Certainly, purposeful reading and reading for meaning were important intentions of the basal reading programs used in the schools I visited. In fact, they were perhaps the most commonly and most forcefully presented goals of the reading programs used in the classrooms I studied. Yet, the relationship between classroom instruction and purposes for reading given by the first-graders was for the most part task-oriented. When compared to their more personal purposes for reading, it was deeply disturbing and forced me to ask the question, "Why"?

Perhaps the answer lies with the type of instruction typically utilized in basal-oriented first-grade classrooms. Take the following typical instructional scenario, for example:

Several students are sitting in a circle reading a story from their basal reader with their teacher.

Teacher: This a story about a family that has to move. Open your books to page 22. Read pages 22 and 23 to find out who Pedro is and why Ramon has to leave him. Fold your hands when you are finished reading so I know when to move on with the lesson.

Teacher: (Pause—students' hands are folded.) Who is Pedro? Why does Ramon have to leave him? Judy, what do you think?

Judy: Pedro is a naughty boy, and Ramon's parents will not let them play together.

Teacher: Very good! (The teacher presented two new questions.) Now read pages 24 and 25. (This process continues until the end of the story.)

Most often, teachers and students in this study followed this procedure on a weekly basis throughout the school year. The questions asked were written verbatim under sections in the guidebook called "Purpose Setting" or "Purposeful Reading." Children in the first grade were expected to do a great deal of this type of instructional reading, as part of their "job" as a student. Often, this reading involved activities that were not specifically related to any personal experience of the student, as illustrated here. The activities were often ends in themselves. Even though a purpose, such as "Read pages 22 and 23 to find out who Pedro is," was mentioned by the teacher in the prereading stage of a story, one could not assume the child understood the stated purpose *as* a purpose. In other words, the purpose stated in the teacher's manual might have little to do with why a child is personally reading the story. It is little wonder with this type of lock-step instruction that educators might erroneously conclude that some first-graders demonstrate limited purposes for reading.

My goal in providing this example of instruction and its accompanying criticism is not to suggest that this is all that I observed or that every first-grade teacher instructed in this way every day. I also observed some teachers modifying published reading materials to best meet the unique needs of their students. Rather, I offer the example as a reminder to teachers of the sterility of what is often found in published lesson plans and teachers' guides when it comes to purpose setting and comprehension development. As one alternative, prediction may be a useful strategy for setting a purpose for reading. Frank Smith discusses the importance of prediction, which he defines as "the prior elimination of unlikely alternatives" (1983, p. 28). That is, readers use their prior knowledge to speculate about the meaning of a message. Currently, many teachers are moving toward this prediction/prove strategy. A sincere question—"What do you think will happen next? or "What do you think this chapter may be trying to explain?"—might be helpful to students. Teachers can encourage these predictions by reading parts of the story, discussing the title, or showing interesting pictures. I would strongly caution teachers, however, to use purpose-setting questions provided by others who don't know their classrooms and their students sparingly, as these are highly impersonal. Predetermined questions are no substitute for questions or discussion initiated by students and teachers, as co-learners, as they read together to find out what they are interested in knowing.

Yes, first-graders develop instructionally oriented purposes for reading that often have little to do with their lives and their personal reasons for reading. Kevin, whom we met at the beginning of the chapter, demonstrated that he clearly understood a variety of purposes for reading. Few would argue that the instruction-oriented purposes given in a manual are insignificant when compared to his own personal purposes for reading. Frank Smith (1990) stresses the importance of purposeful, relevant reading and writing when he states, "Reading and writing are two activities that promote thought—provided that what is read is worth thinking about and that writing is used for extending the imagination of the writer" (p. 128).

Fortunately, the children in this study shared far more personal purposes for reading than instructional purposes. These purposes seem to have their origins both inside and outside of the classroom.

Not all first-grade reading instruction observed in this study was conducted in reading groups using basal reading materials. Numerous other less structured reading activities took place throughout the day. For example, those children who had completed both reading group and seatwork were often allowed to read books of their choice either from home, the library, or a collection in the classroom. Many children took advantage of this opportunity to read, as the children phrased it, "just for fun." One teacher had a "reading park" in the back of her room filled with books, comfortable chairs, and nice thick carpeting for children to use during their free time. When children had completed all of their seatwork, they would stretch out in the "park" with a good book and read. The children would often chuckle if a story was amusing, and they enjoyed sharing different parts of the book with a friend. Other teachers had set times each day in which children and teacher sat and read for sheer enjoyment, either independently or as a group.

Many of the children in the classroom with the "reading park" included reading as a means to occupy leisure time in an enjoyable way in their statements regarding why they read. Kathy told me, "I love to lay on the rug in the 'park' and read books. Reading helps me relax." Christine echoed this comment as she stated, "I love to go to the 'park' and read *Curious George* when my work is all done."

Other first-graders' understandings of why they read were associated with story reading by their teachers and the school librarian. As Seth remarked:

When my teacher reads to us. That's what I'm learning to read for. Like sometimes during the story I pretend I'm the one. Like the person in the book. Then something good happens to me, or I'm the hero. That's why I'm reading. When I can read the book, I can be in the story.

Or, as Peggy stated:

Our library teacher makes stories like a game. She talks to you about them before she reads. Then when you get to the part she talked about you almost know what happened. But not always. Sometimes she fools us. Then we think it's funny and laugh. With her reading is like watching TV and pretending it's real. I like this kind of reading. You don't have to worry about the words or the questions.

Both Seth and Peggy have developed a "reading as recreation" understanding of what reading is all about. Each of their perceptions seems to be highly positive, and in each case the perception is associated with a teaching practice. Clearly, not all first-grade reading instruction is the mechanical, purpose-setting, question-and-answer regimen of the basal reader associated with task-oriented purposes for reading. The positive perceptions of Seth and Peggy stem from the pleasurable activity of listening to a story, an activity that enables children to respond and interact with the story on a personal level which seems to be key in the development of meaningful purposes for reading.

Indeed, purposes for reading take on a variety of forms. It is clear that school reading experiences, both structured and unstructured, contribute to these identities. Even though most of the classroom reading instruction observed was formal, structured purposes for reading do not seem to dominate children's perceptions of purposes. Other school reading experiences, such as storytime and library visits, seem to influence perceptions as well.

Many children, like Seth and Peggy, talked about reading as an enjoyable way to occupy leisure time. Michelle said, "It's important to read. There are a lot of good stories out there." Chris found reading to be a soothing activity. He stated, "Sometimes I read all by myself. That's fun and relaxing. I always do that every night. It makes me want to go to sleep." Mike felt, "It's important to read because it would be bad to grow up and not be able to read nice stories to your own kids. I want to read books to children for fun when I grow up."

One cannot be certain how these children came to these understandings, but it is clear that they see reading as relaxing and soothing. Research has shown that children can see reading as a source of comfort at an extremely early age. One 3-year-old who suffered from a variety of painful physical ailments was observed settling herself on a couch with a rag doll and a pile of books, and was heard to say, "Now I can read to Looby Lou, 'cause she's tired and sad, and she needs a cuddle and a bottle and a book" (Butler, 1979, p. 102). Again, we see the total absence of any connection between these types of understandings and the purpose-setting instructional activities commonly encountered in structured reading programs. The children know the difference between "Teacher's Edition" questions and ones to which the teacher is truly interested in hearing their responses.

In addition to recreational reading purposes, children identified purposes that were information-driven. That is, they clearly stated that they read to find out specific information or learn "new things." Chris was a first-grader who seemed to possess a clear understanding of why he reads: "I read because it helps me learn new things. You can learn about space. I love learning about space, and I like to learn to do new experiments, too." Casey, another first-grader in a different classroom, had a similar purpose for reading. "I read books to learn new things. It's fun to read because it is fun to learn. It's very important to learn new things to get along in the world."

It is impossible to know the origin or evolution of these understandings. Perhaps they are echoes of a teacher's words, or maybe a parent's or grandparent's. Perhaps these first-graders came to this point without the help of a teacher or relative. Whatever the origin, it is important not only to recognize the validity of the children's perceptions, but also to capitalize on their interest and enthusiasm in classroom settings. Chris and Casey are clearly excited about learning new information that has special meaning to each of them. It would be tragic if this interest and enthusiasm were dampened by force-feeding them a steady diet of seemingly artificial purposes for reading found in the pages of a teacher's manual. Children's reading development may not be enhanced by being told to read pages 22 and 23 to find out "who Pedro is and why Ramon is forced to leave." Instead, why not let *them* ask the questions that will engage them in a personalized and exciting discussion about the new information they have learned. We must begin asking about and valuing the purposes children set for themselves as they begin reading. Once again, this can only be done by listening to children and taking our cues from them. After a few opening paragraphs of a story, we might simply ask, "What do you want to find out?"

Some first-graders also discussed how reading helped them to interact with their surroundings. Indeed, they demonstrated an understanding of the role reading plays in our society. As Victor stated, "I want to learn to read so I know how to read maps and the signs on the road, so I know which way to go. You need to read newspapers to find out what is happening in the world." Jack agreed and felt, "It's important to learn to read so you can read signs and stuff. I can read the word EXIT. I know what it means, too."

Once again, it is impossible to know precisely how these perceptions developed. Perhaps a caring parent or enlightened teacher helped these boys to come to this point. Or it could just as well have been Mr. Rogers, or Maria on "Sesame Street," who first planted the seed of understanding as to how reading fits in a society that demands literacy skills.

My study clearly identified several different purposes for reading. Some students identified informational or environmental purposes, and others identified recreational or instructional purposes. The purposes generated by first-graders were in no way confused, immature, incomplete, or lacking. Rather, children's perceptions were sometimes all too accurate regarding limiting instructional purposes such as, "Reading is to pass first grade." For the most part, they were clearly meaning-driven and demonstrated that these beginning readers were sensitive to their environment and the role played by reading within it. These rich perceptions can be connected to both home and school experiences and appear to be the result of parents and/or teachers helping children to connect reading with the world in which they live. This finding is inconsistent with earlier research which reports that many first-graders express little or no logical purpose for reading (Denny & Weintraub, 1966).

This study suggests that children *do* understand various purposes for reading. With this in mind, it seems that efforts expended in helping children connect reading with everyday experiences and with their personal needs will pay rich dividends in making reading meaningful.

A Classroom Teacher Responds...

It was basal reader characters like Pedro and Ramon who forced me to consider who was really in charge of reading instruction in my classroom. Day in and day out, the writers of our reading textbook provided a reason for reading each and every page of the basal stories. Those writers seemed convinced of the necessity of asking purpose-setting questions ("Why was Pedro late for school?" "What did Ramon eat for lunch?"), and I rarely questioned them. But did the children in my classroom really care? Was this a sensible reason to ask my students to read this story? I had come to know instinctively that questions like these had nothing to do with purposeful reading, but it was reassuring to receive confirmation of this through the real-life purposes for reading that the children divulged in this study.

This chapter really hit home for me. It seemed as if the children interviewed saw reading as two separate entities. They discussed what we would consider school or "instructional reading" as reading, the only purpose of which was to keep them busy, help them do seatwork, or pass first grade. On the other hand, they viewed reading at home, in the library, or during free time as pleasurable, relaxing, and informative. I find this dichotomy distressing. Who is in charge of reading in our classrooms? Aren't we, as teachers, unwittingly responsible for changing our students' very personal purposes for reading to trite instructional purposes? Children's reasons for reading are rich, personal, and important. We must respect the children's views on why they read, and then build on them. I am increasingly comfortable with the idea of providing many books for my students and letting them generate, and at times share with me, their own purposes for reading. After reading the children's comments, I am now concerned that an overreliance on preplanned purpose setting will not only cause children to forsake their personal reasons for reading, but also impose an unnatural dependency on the teacher's reason for reading. Wouldn't it be unfortunate if our students had no purpose for reading unless we suggested one?

I do believe in setting the stage or focusing a child's attention before reading a particular story or group of stories relating to a theme or unit of study. For example, if my theme is winter animals, the purposes for reading related stories, articles, and poems might include reading for specific information, enjoyment, and general knowledge. It isn't necessary for me to pinpoint the purpose for reading each text or each page of every story. It is, however, important for me and my students to have our own personal reasons for reading.

This study suggests that children come to us in first grade with valuable reasons to read: to enjoy, to learn, to interact. As a teacher and a parent, I can't think of any better purposes for reading. I concur that we should listen to our students, respect their needs, and facilitate instruction that closes the gap between reading as an instructional/school activity and reading as a natural, real-life experience.

Parents Respond...

Our children have exhibited a number of reasons for wanting to read successfully. The reasons include those enumerated by the author: for recreation, to understand their environment or surroundings, to obtain information, to please a parent, to do well in school. But we also have observed another important reason. Our children seem to realize that reading gives them the power to function one on one with adults and older siblings on their turf. This power was no more evident than when they first comprehended that they could read street signs, billboards, and store signs. Our children were smugly happy when they read food container labels, junk mail advertisements, or the words on the screen accompanying television ads. Like many parents, we have tried to reinforce this awareness of entry into the adult reading world (and tried to maintain a little sanity!) by playing a game on car trips where we search together for words on signs beginning with each letter of the alphabet in turn.

Perhaps for all the reasons stated here, our children have shown a strong desire to master the art of reading as they have gone through first grade. On the basis of papers and books brought home and their feedback at storytime before bed, it appears that our children's first-grade teachers have been able to maintain and enhance their desire to become readers. We are lucky in that none of our children had significant problems learning to read, which might have made a difference in their attitudes. We do not know exactly what their teachers do in the classroom for purpose setting. But we do know that there was a lot of caring for our kids and also a lot of personal interaction. We'd almost guarantee that the "Ramon and Pedro" approach to purpose setting would have negligible results with our children and that the "prediction/prove" strategy would work for them. We hope that this method is becoming more prevalent!

▶ 6

Reading Groups:
Hard Cover/
Soft Cover

PREVIEW

This chapter will help you to see that first-graders have an accurate sense of how well they are doing in reading at school. It dispels the commonly held belief that young children are currently protected from this information through use of discreet reading group labels. The chapter illustrates how first-graders develop a sense of how well they are doing in school based on signals such as reading group placement and the books they read. You will also see differences in how first-graders who are placed in high and low reading groups think about themselves as learners and how those feelings change dramatically over time.

After reading this chapter, you will see the importance of encouraging children to share their feelings about how they are doing in school. You may be less likely to view this as noninstructional time, as this practice can be as important as anything you might do throughout your instructional day. Listening to children is well worth the time; it is a necessary component of good teaching.

SARAH'S IN A HARD-COVER BOOK

The two first-grade girls screamed excitedly as they ran across the rain-soaked parking lot to where Sarah's mother was waiting in the car. Sarah was dragging her friend Marsha by the hand and was clearly happy to be out of school for the day. No sooner was Sarah in the car than she blurted out the good news:

I'm reading a hard-cover book! I got a new hard-cover reading book. Mrs. Smith said I am doing just great in reading now. My end-of-the-book test was almost perfect, and if I keep doing this well, pretty soon I'll get to be in the "high group."

Sarah's mother was excited:

Honey, that's wonderful! I'm so proud of you. I can't believe you've gone through all those books in just the first three months of school. I knew you could do it. I know you are working hard. Your Dad and I are very, very proud of you.

Marsha was uncharacteristically quiet through the whole exchange. Finally, and with some degree of reservation, she took a drawing from her book bag and tentatively offered it to Mrs. Williams. "See what we did in art today? The art teacher said I'm one of the finest artists in the class." Sarah's mother looked at the drawing and was effusive in her praise of Marsha. "Honey, that's very, very good. Look at that sky. Isn't that nice? You have done a wonderful drawing. Your mother will be proud of you." Marsha, her confidence restored, tentatively offered:

I like my reading group. Mrs. Smith says I'm doing pretty good too, and if I keep working hard, pretty soon I'll be in a hard-cover book, too. Jason still isn't reading too good yet, and Mrs. Smith said that he's going to get to go to see Mr. Quaker, the reading teacher. Jason's in the "Rainbow" group now, but he might be back in our group pretty soon.

The topic of conversation then shifted to giggles and laughs as the girls became distracted by a second-grade boy who dropped half of his papers in one of the puddles. That seemed to be the highlight of the day for both girls.

That night, Sarah had another chance to talk about her hard-cover reading book. At dinner her mother gave Sarah a sly little wink and said, "Honey, why don't you tell Dad about your new reading book."

Sarah seized the opportunity like a frog on a June bug. "Dad, I'm reading in a hard-cover book."

Her father seemed very pleased with that notion. He commented, "That's great, sweetheart. That's great. Did you move to a different reading group, too?"

"Aw, no, I'm still in the 'Boxcar Children' group."

"That's O.K. I know pretty soon you will be in the 'Orangemen.' When did Willis get put into the 'Orangemen'?"

Sarah replied, "I don't really remember. But Michael used to be in my group in kindergarten, too, and now he's in the 'Orangemen' too."

Sarah's father replied, "I'm sure if you keep working hard, you'll be back with Michael and Willis soon. I know you can do it, Honey. I'm so proud of you."

That night, after Sarah had gone to bed, the Williamses had a chance to talk more about her progress in school. "Seems like Sarah's getting back on track," remarked Mr. Williams.

"Yes, I think she is doing very well," Sarah's mother replied.

"What happened to her, anyhow? Why did she get put in that middle reading group after kindergarten?"

"From what the teacher said, her placement test really wasn't quite where it should have been." Sarah's father seemed puzzled and commented, "That seems kind of hard to believe. You know, she and Michael went through the same nursery school program, and she always did a lot better than Michael. As far as I know, she did better in kindergarten as well."

"Well, she seems to be doing fine now, and pretty soon I think she'll be caught up again."

"Well, I hope so. I just don't want her to fall behind like Mitch's little guy did. You remember what happened to him."

Sometimes it is surprising to find how much young children know without being told. Although Mrs. Smith does not use the terms *high* and *low* group with Sarah, and her parents are careful to discuss her progress after she is in bed, Sarah clearly has an understanding of how she is doing in school. It is as if children have a sixth sense or some sort of radar antenna designed especially for the purpose of providing them with information that adults would prefer they not have. They seem to know about surprises, presents, and parties before they occur, as well as knowing when Mom's about to be laid off from her job or when a relative's illness is serious. Luckily, this same sixth sense seems to tell them when to keep quiet about the surprise party or not to trouble Mom or Dad just yet with questions about Grandpa being very sick or the impending layoff at the plant. In spite of their high activity level and what sometimes seems like incessant chatter, young children are keen observers of the world around them. They seem to be particularly adept at piercing the protective shield some teachers employ in an attempt to protect their students from the hard, cold truth about how they are doing in school.

CHILDREN'S PERCEPTIONS: HOW AM I DOING?

Interview after interview in my study indicated that first-graders know how they are doing in school, and that this knowledge grows and develops over time. Reading group names like "Bluebirds," "Muppets," and "Cowboys" do nothing to change the fact that there is a high group made up of "smart" readers, a middle group made up of "not so smart" children, and a low group made up of children who are "not smart" at all. Although we as teachers and parents know that a child can be very bright and still experience difficulty in reading, children usually do not; they often equate reading ability with "being smart" and reading difficulty with "being dumb," whether they are referring to themselves or others. Even in the settings where groups were nonexistent, the children were able to articulate how well they were doing and frequently viewed reading performance as an index of self-worth.

Despite some teachers' attempts to protect children's self-esteem and/or present a positively reinforcing learning environment, first-graders possess a definite sense of how things are going for them in reading. As one teacher, who typifies the myth of the protective shield, explained, "I told Julie she was going to special reading because she was such a good worker, and Mr. G. needed help with the other children. I didn't want her to feel badly about needing the extra help." Julie's explanation, however, was quite different. When we were talking on the playground, she said:

> *Reading is very hard for me. I can see I'm not as good a reader as most of the kids in the class. I really am trying and Mr. G. is helping me to be a good reader. He's awesome. If I don't know a word, he just tells me. He says there's no sense getting frustrated.*

Julie, in spite of her teacher's attempt to protect her, is well aware of her difficulty in reading. Tara and Douglas visited with me one day on the playground, and they spoke about reading groups. They were able to articulate how hard- and soft-cover books were the key to understanding the high/low reading group mystery:

> *We started off with an easy book. Then we went to an easy book, but a little harder, but it still had a soft cover. A hard book has a hard cover and an easy book has a soft cover. That's how you tell if someone is in a high reading group. But the teacher just calls us Red, Blue, and Green. If you have a hard book you are a good reader. Green is still in a soft book so they are not good readers. Those are baby books.*

Other interviews with first-graders confirmed that hard-cover books were a real status symbol among the children. Doug was obviously pleased with himself when he remarked:

> *I read to my dad and brother last night. It was* The Three Billy Goats Gruff. *Excellent book! I stayed up until 8:00 reading. We read a story called "Dave's Day" in our reading book today. I've read so many stories. Did you notice I'm in a hard-cover book?*

Of course, I reassured him that it was one of the first things I had noticed.

But the clues to reading progress go beyond the obvious soft and hard covers of their primers. First-graders have also come to understand that full pages of texts with no pictures are an index of the difficulty level of a book, and that this, too, is connected with how well they are doing. In fact, full pages of text, like hard covers, are often viewed as a status symbol. As Beth explained, "This is a hard book 'cuz it has lots of pages with all words and no pictures. You can see I'm the best reader in the whole class." Tommy was out to impress his older brother and friends as he said to the librarian:

> *I need to take out a book with lots of words but no pictures. One that doesn't even have a picture on the cover. I want my brother and his friends to know I am a good reader. They are in third grade.*

Clearly, these examples enable us to see that first-graders possess a definite sense of how they are doing in reading at school. They have come to understand many strategies for monitoring their own reading progress, such as "what book they are in," "whether it has a soft cover or a hard cover," "if it is fat or thin," or whether it is "full of pictures or just words."

Of all the categories of reading perceptions reported by first-graders, those perceptions dealing with how well they are doing are perhaps the most obviously related to the classroom context. Indeed, a continuous "How am I doing?" feedback loop seems to exist in first-grade classrooms. This feedback and reinforcement loop keeps beginning readers continually apprised of how they are doing in reading and permits them to understand that progress in reading is often gauged by successfully moving through a series of books and eventually entering the status symbol of first grade—a hard-cover primer. The system helps them to recognize that reading groups are fast, medium, and slow as well as Red, Blue, and Green, and ultimately it enables them to measure themselves against their peers.

Observations indicated that first-grade teachers deliver a constant flow of feedback to their students. Some teachers stamp hands with "Excellent," others stamp children's papers when they know all their reading words or can recognize their letters with no errors; other teachers put stars on envelopes for good work, and some apply stickers after enough stars are earned. Teachers are extremely generous with their praise. Phrases like "Good job," "I'm proud of you," and "I'm so pleased with you," are almost automatic responses to good behavior and correct answers.

It appears that it is almost impossible for a first-grader to get through a day without positive and/or negative feedback. The negative feedback is generally as pointed as the positive, as one boy who missed a word from his list found out when he was told, "I can't give you a stamp because you missed a word," or the child who banged her hand on the desk out of frustration after she got a "warning" for not working.

Even the principal got into the feedback act when she visited a first-grade classroom and remarked to the teacher and class, "These people are very good. I had no idea they knew all of these words." One child came back to me when the principal left, shrugged her shoulders, and appeared to dismiss the compliment as she informed me, "She says everything is good."

Progress is heavily emphasized in first-grade classrooms, particularly progress in reading. Comments such as, "Once you know all of these words you can move on to the next book," "We're trying to get ready for second grade," and "You need to know these words a little bit better before you can go into the preprimer" serve constantly to remind children of the progress they are expected to demonstrate. Remarks such as, "You'll learn them fast because you are a smart little girl" add a "smart/not smart" element to the rate of progress scenario.

There is little question that a "How am I doing?" monitoring system exists in first-grade classrooms, and it is not surprising that even beginning first-graders are aware of how things are going for them in school. As Jeremy boasted, "I'm one of the best readers in the whole class," and Andrea explained apologetically, "My group is still in readiness. That's bad."

How well things are going can also have an effect on how these children feel about themselves as learners. Emotions run the full gamut from negative ("There's a lot I can't read" or "I'm not a good reader") to positive ("I feel good when I'm reading," and "I'm a good reader 'cuz my teacher tells me how to sound letters out"). Other feelings involve more reflection. An hour after he finished his first conversation with me, Danny, a first-grade repeater, came back to where I was talking to other children and offered to tell me more about reading. I encouraged him to tell me more, and after what seemed to be an eternity he offered the following:

> *I don't like to read because I can't read most of the words. They're a little too big and a little too long. I like when my Mom reads to me and my sister. Thinking about reading makes me feel uncomfortable. I'm not good at it. I like to think about my farm. I know everything about that.*

Bonnie was a first-grader who also seemed to be concerned. She explained that she goes to special reading class every day because "the other kids in the class read a lot better than me. They know lots of words and can make the right sounds. I'm not a very good reader in school."

Reading can be viewed as a monumental task requiring Herculean effort as well. As first-grader Jeremy put it:

> *I read either 100 or 2,000 books once in one day. I was awful thirsty after reading that many books. But there were some short books. I only kinda know how to read. I have trouble reading.*

That's effort! The responses children made about how reading makes them feel were spontaneous. They were not directly asked, "How do you feel about reading?" Feelings emerged naturally in the context of talking about reading.

FEELINGS CHANGE OVER TIME

These feelings sometimes changed over time. It is interesting to note that almost all of the first-graders who had been placed in the highest reading groups at the beginning of the school year (September) did not identify themselves as good readers. They talked about becoming readers and often compared themselves to adult readers. Tim commented, "I'm not really a good reader 'cuz I can't read lots of stuff yet," or, as Max said, "I'm not a very good reader. I can't read everything. I'm just learning." Erin felt that she didn't know how to read yet, in spite of the fact that she read daily. "I don't know how to read very well, but I read every day. I'm not a good reader. I only know how to read some books at home and everything at school. I don't know how to read every book." Jeremy, another child who had been placed in the highest reading group, said, "I don't know how to read really good. I'm not a good reader. To read really good you have to get to know all the words." These children, when interviewed at the beginning of the school year, seemed to view reading as an all-or-nothing endeavor. To be a good reader, they must know it all.

When these children were interviewed in May, their feelings had changed dramatically. By this time, these students were feeling quite good about themselves as readers. Tim proudly commented:

> *I love being in the best group. We get the end-of-book tests perfect. We aren't in regular reading books. We're in whole language, but we still get perfect on the tests.*

As Max confidently stated:

> *I'm in the highest reading group in school and a very good reader. I can read everything. Even the tests we took in school were easy to read, and the teacher said they would be hard. They were simple.*

Erin commented:

> *I'm a good reader and even read books at night to my sister. I can even read the books that my mother has out on the table, and they're grown up books. I love to read, but sometimes I can't find books I like.*

Jeremy's feelings as a reader had changed, as he stated: "I'm one of the best readers in the whole class, and that's pretty good."

The story is quite different for those children who have been placed in the lower reading groups. At the beginning of the year, all of these children appeared quite confident in their reading ability and referred to themselves as good readers. John told me, "I am a good reader and already know how to read. No one reads to me at home, but I read to myself." Julie said, "I can read books. I go to the library and get big girl books, not baby books. My mother lets me. I get to play games and say my ABC's in reading. I am a good reader." Terry explained, "I am a good reader. I look at the pictures, and that helps me read the story."

By the end of the school year, these children felt quite differently about reading and about themselves as readers. John stated emphatically, "I hate to read. It's stupid. I can't even sound words out yet. We are still in baby books." Julie's feelings had changed, as well, as she explained:

I have to go for special reading every day because the other kids read better in school than me. They know more words and can make the right sounds. Next week we have to take this test and we only get one and a half minutes to finish it. I get so nervous and can't remember what to do. I know I'm going to fail.

Terry sighed, "I'm in the lowest reading group. That means I can't read good. Our group is the worst in the class."

Yes, first-graders' feelings can and do change over time. As the year progressed, first-graders became cognizant of the scales and yardsticks used in school. "Highest group," "lowest group," "primers," "preprimers," "easy tests," "hard tests," "best reader," and "worst reader" were all terms used at the end of first grade as children spoke of how they felt about themselves and reading.

As these quotations illustrate, children's understandings about how they are doing in reading significantly influence how they feel about reading and about themselves as readers. Emotions run the entire range of feelings from negative to positive, and can sometimes change dramatically over time. These feelings are reflected in first-graders' perceptions of reading. Their reflections frequently suggest that their feelings are shaped by reading events which have occurred in school.

The constant flow of feedback from teachers seems to be partially responsible for how these children feel about themselves as readers. As mentioned earlier, positive feedback is also an integral part of the day-to-day operations of the first-grade classroom. Children enjoy earning stickers to decorate their folders, and they like showing off the "Excellent" stamps on the backs of their hands. As one first grader remarked, "It's nice to get stickers on your work folder. Then you know you are doing good, and so do all the other kids, and your Mom knows too, if she comes to Parents' Night." A little girl proudly showed me the "Excellent" on the back of her ink-stamped hand and stated:

I love it when I get an "Excellent." I like to look at it at my seat. Then I know I'm smart. I try to get one every day. My Mom likes them too. It makes her feel happy when I do good.

But the feedback is not all positive. Sometimes children's actions elicit negative feedback from teachers. Before one reading group began, a teacher approached John and said, "Did you remember your letters today?" John very timidly replied, "No, I lost them." The teacher responded, "Oh no! How do you ever expect to get into the preprimer if you forget your words?" Another child asked the teacher when they would be getting books like the other groups. She replied, "Not for awhile. You are still in readiness. You don't get reading books yet, just workbooks. If we work hard in these you will get reading books." With feedback like this, is it any wonder that first-graders know exactly where they stand and form self-concepts as readers accordingly?

One teacher spent a great deal of time reinforcing all of the good workers at their seats. She constantly reiterated how important it was to be quiet during reading groups. The teacher became distracted by a child as she was trying to teach one of the groups. She said, "Were you talking, Billy? I have to give you a warning. Please don't make me give warnings. I hate to give warnings. Who has warnings today?" She wrote the names of three boys on the blackboard. She then said:

> *You must remember not to talk. We never talk during reading groups. Don't anyone talk to Billy. He is trying hard not to talk. Billy has never earned a sticker for excellent work. I'm sure he would like one. Help the kids with warnings not to talk.*

Negative feedback heavily influences how children feel about reading and how reading makes them feel. Billy told me, "I hate reading. It's so dumb. I'm the worst reader in the class."

It is not as though teachers are unconcerned about children's feelings and self-concepts; on the contrary, they are quite sensitive in this area. As one teacher remarked to a group of parents on Parents' Night, "If your child has a poor self-concept and doesn't feel good about himself, he cannot succeed in school." Teachers often go out of their way to disguise the fact that students are in a low reading group or must leave the room for special help. The teachers involved in this study truly tried to protect their students from negative feedback. In discussing this with the teachers, it became apparent that negative comments seem to stem, instead, from the tremendous amount of pressure to "cover" the first-grade reading program. As one teacher lamented after she had just finished giving her students good morning hugs and attention, "I wish I could have more of this kind of time with my kids. It feels so good. But there's just so much to cover that there is no time for anything else." Or as another teacher complained:

> *Why are there so many books to do in the first grade? If we don't read a story each day my kids won't be on grade level. Just once, I would like to feel comfortable reading any book we wanted to. You can imagine what the second-grade teachers would be saying then. Even now, they are always complaining that the kids aren't ready when they get to second grade.*

Indeed, all the teachers I interviewed echoed the same emotion: "There is too much to get done and so little time to do it in."

It is reasonable to conclude that all of these pressures can lead to children's frustration and negative feelings about reading and about themselves in the context of reading. However, all is not doom and gloom; many of the first-graders interviewed remained positive throughout their first grade experience and were very proud of their accomplishments as readers. This is understandable when one considers that much of the feedback that exists in first-grade classrooms is positive and that some children have done the comparing and found out they're the best. "Good work," "Nice job," "Excellent," and "I'm proud of you" feedback statements are part and parcel of first-grade classrooms. It is important to consider, however, that there are a number of students whose first-grade experience is unsuccessful and who, at an early age, have deemed reading as "stupid" and themselves as failures.

The finding that first-graders demonstrated an understanding of reading status, as defined by "what book they were in," is not unique to this study. A study of first-graders' perceptions of reading and writing reported similar findings (Boljonis & Hinchman, 1987). The fact that hard-cover books are important status symbols among first-graders should not surprise us at all. Is there a reader among us who did not feel the same as a child? What was surprising, however, was how precisely the children could position themselves in the early reader progression and its attendant status.

Of all the categories of reading perceptions reported by first-graders, those perceptions dealing with "how well they are doing" are perhaps the most directly related to the classroom environment. Positive and negative feedback is an integral part of the day-to-day operations of first-grade classrooms. Stamps and stars for good work and loss of playtime and verbal reprimands for poor work help keep beginning readers continually apprised of how they are doing in reading. Given this system, it is inescapable.

How children think they are doing seems to affect how they feel about themselves and reading. In short, a child's sense of self-worth appears to be directly affected by reading group performance. Emotions run the full spectrum and can change over time. It was observed that, as the year progressed, children became much more aware of the scales and yardsticks used in schools, and their feelings about themselves and reading often changed dramatically. As mentioned earlier, many first-graders placed in the highest reading group at the beginning of the year did not identify themselves as good readers, but by the end of the year they were feeling very positive about themselves. In sharp contrast, children placed in the lowest reading group appeared quite confident in their reading ability at the beginning of the year, but by the end of the year had negative opinions about themselves as readers.

First-graders, regardless of ability, become aware of scholastic yardsticks, and these yardsticks clearly color their perceptions of themselves as readers. Sadly, some children's experiences in school convinced them that they are not good readers. In some cases, this appears to affect general self-concept dramatically.

The first-grade teachers who participated in this study indicated that they often attempted to protect children's self-esteem and present a positively reinforcing learning environment. They cited examples of how they used reading group names such as "Carebears" in an effort to keep children from knowing if their reading group was high, medium, or low. The very effort they go through to create this neutral environment, however, seems counterproductive. It appears to focus children's attention on the differences, as if there is something to be hidden and thus found out.

When one of the teachers in this study finished reading a draft of this chapter, she registered surprise and remarked, "It looks like I'd be closer to achieving my goal if I didn't try to protect the kids from the realities of grouping. I guess they know where they are anyway. I might as well stop trying to kid them. That only seems to make things worse." Once again, we find that first-graders know a great deal more about reading in the classroom than we often give them credit for. More important, however, this study shows that many of the experiences that some children encounter in first grade undermine their self-esteem and make them feel negative about themselves and about reading.

Teachers need to exercise caution as they formulate reading groups. Research has suggested that instructional and social reading experiences differ dramatically for students participating in high and low reading groups, thus affecting student learning (Allington, 1983; Hiebert, 1983). Regardless of what a group was labeled, the children in this study had a keen awareness of their placement in terms of achievement. Furthermore, reading group assignment seemed to become a symbol of general academic competence for both teachers and their students. For example, many children in the lowest reading group indicated that they had to have all their seatwork checked daily by a student in a higher reading group "to make sure it was done right" before turning it in to the teacher. One first-grader complained, "It isn't fair just because Erika's in the best reading group that she looks at my work. She isn't the teacher." Benjamin simply explained, "When my work is done, Terri has to look at it. She's in the 'Dodgers.'" When I asked Benjamin to explain why Terri looked at his work, he said, "Because she is in a high reading group and they can do all the work real good."

This chapter is not an argument for or against one particular type of reading group instruction. Rather, it is intended to show that children do develop a deep understanding of how well they are doing in reading at school. I believe we must listen to children, regardless of what type of reading group experience a child encounters. Listening to children will help us better understand how they are feeling about themselves as learners and readers. Through listening, we may have the information necessary to experiment with different groupings, adjusting accordingly, in order to find what works best for the children. Because children have unique learning styles and each classroom has a distinctive classroom mixture, various grouping patterns may become necessary.

Although most teachers continue to use ability grouping, some are currently using different forms of heterogeneous grouping, such as cooperative learning, where a small group of children form a cooperative group that works together to solve a problem or complete a task; they report that children who had typically experienced difficulty in reading are much more eager to read. According to Regie Routman in *Transitions from Literature to Literacy* (1988), flexibility is critical if ability grouping is used. She asserts that it is "...important not to keep the children in the same grouping structure all year. Flexibility is necessary so children learn to interact with all their peers and so they don't become 'slotted'" (p. 126). She further recommends that, in addition to ability grouping, children can be grouped according to peers they would like to be grouped with, according to interest, or according to skill need. Whole-class reading instruction is another method that is currently being used in some classrooms. However, Routman warns teachers against using whole-class grouping on a regular basis, as it limits discussion where all students have the opportunity to become involved and respond critically.

Clearly, there is no single best way to group for instruction, just as there is no one best way to teach reading to all children. I maintain, however, that within any given classroom, a best fit exists between a given child and an instructional group. The way to find the best fit is to listen to children and remain flexible in your grouping.

A Classroom Teacher Responds...

Through the candid words of the children, this chapter helped me realize that I must rethink some of my current reading group practices. As a parent, I know how rarely I was able to trick my 4-year-old into an early bedtime or eating a nutritious vegetable that I had disguised with applesauce or mashed potatoes. As teachers, we should also realize that we have little success in disguising the academic status of our students. Children do have a keen awareness of their own abilities, and perhaps we need to do more to enhance this ability rather than hide any lack of ability.

Reading groups, as described in this study, may not be the best way to provide instruction for all children. What I am uncomfortable with as a result of what the children said is the usual permanence of first-grade reading groups. I have witnessed children who "fell behind" in the first few months of first grade, never to catch up with the system. Year after year, they are placed in the lowest reading group because they haven't completed last year's book. After reading how many of these first-graders feel about themselves as readers, I felt increasingly uncomfortable.

The children in the study prompted many questions for me. I began to think about how easy it is to get caught up in the reporting system if we adhere strictly to the basal reader approach. Do we really need to cover every story, every worksheet, and every skill in the workbook? For some reason, especially with increasing accountability, we often feel safer doing this. At least we can say we taught it, and we feel we have "proof." To be truly accountable as teachers, however, perhaps it is more important to assess the children informally on a regular basis rather than focusing solely on end-of-book tests. Maybe it is time to replace the published end-of-book tests with informal reading inventories, to keep running records of children's reading progress, and to listen to their individual assessment of how they are doing. Perhaps, as we listen to them talk about books and authors they love, there will be less concentration on what group they are in and on how they compare to others.

I have always known that children learn to read at different rates and through different learning styles. Children learn to read over a much longer time span than the September-through-June time frame that so many parents and teachers believe in. Beginning reading instruction must therefore be flexible and fun. Within the same group, children of varying abilities can demonstrate strengths and learn new concepts. The child who is less proficient in letter–sound correspondence may outshine his phonetic counterpart when matching opposites or brainstorming rhyming words. The visual learner in the group may easily identify a sight word in a big book, but the auditory learner may be the group member to distinguish the rhyming pattern in the story. If we begin to "informalize" our formal reading instruction, it might result in more meaningful reading experiences for all students. Rather than creating a "good reader/bad reader" atmosphere, we might help children better understand their strengths as well as their weaknesses and help them utilize this information as they become successful readers.

As a result of reading how aware the children are of their progress, I am going to continue implementing some whole-group reading instruction around thematic units, and provide flexible groups when necessary to work on specific skills or projects or interests. The reading materials will center around books, articles, poems, and lyrics to meaningful songs. I hope my "reading groups" and reading instruction will continue to change, as each year I will have new students with different needs and interests. What will not change, however, is my awareness that all children must feel successful and be successful as they learn to read.

Parents Respond...

It is patently obvious to any parent that children can sense how they are doing vis-à-vis their peers almost from the time they begin to interact socially as preschoolers. Whether it be playing with other kids in the neighborhood or working at school, they instinctively know when something is tougher for one child than another. They receive and understand a myriad of signals. On the playground or the soccer field, they can tell who is coordinated and who is not.

In school, they hear one child struggle reading aloud in reading group while another does not. They quickly comprehend that one group's reading book is more difficult than another's.

We would wager that the ability to discern individual status, strengths and weaknesses versus peers is so ingrained that it is a basic human (indeed animal!) instinct. Some researchers probably concluded long ago that this skill dates back to prehistoric times, when such knowledge was important for survival itself.

Because children are able to tell how they are doing in class, it would seem neither necessary nor desirable for teachers to try to hide the fact from their students that we are all learning at our own rate and in our own way. Kids can be encouraged not to measure their progress against others but, rather, to feel proud of their own progress and accomplishments. One such approach to which our children have responded well as first-graders is called "Bones and Feathers." Early in the year, each child draws a large face of a dog, gives the dog a name, and pins the dog's face on the bulletin board. For some period of time thereafter, every time the child reads a book at home or has a book read by a parent or sibling, the name of the book is written inside an outline drawing of a bone (photocopies of which are supplied by the teacher), and the bone is brought to school and pinned next to the child's dog face. Before the autumn ends, all the dogs are surrounded by many, many bones. Later in the year, in a similar activity, the dog is replaced by a bird and the bones by feathers. This time the names of books read by the children themselves are written within the outline of the feather.

We agree with the author that it is very important in dealing with children and their performance not to denigrate and thereby demotivate them. This is especially true given that, as the author notes, each child develops differently. Children's lightbulbs "click on" at some point. Once this happens, their progress is rapid, and their appetite for reading often becomes voracious. A good teacher will see when the individual student's lightbulb turns on and will adjust reading group assignments and other activities as appropriate to take advantage of the child's sudden ability to progress rapidly.

We have had two children complete the first-grade experience; our third and youngest child now is midway through first grade. One of the two older children moved up to another reading group midyear. The other had the opposite experience; she was selected for Chapter 1 assistance during her first-grade year. Although we as parents initially viewed her entry into the remedial reading program with alarm and dismay, she thrived on the individual attention she received from an extremely caring and talented teacher. Her personality always has required acceptance, support, and attention. Before the end of second grade, she was among the top readers in her class. We shudder to think what would have happened to her if the "problem" had not been identified early on and addressed in a straightforward manner that built self-esteem.

▶ 7

Standardized Test Time: Get a Good Night's Sleep

PREVIEW

In the two previous chapters you saw that a relationship exists between teaching practices and how children think about reading in school. In this chapter, you will see that instructional practices influence how children come to understand standardized test situations. This chapter will also provide you with insights into ways parents and teachers of first-graders view testing.

After reading this chapter, you may be more effective in testing reading in your classroom. You will see how you can use student feedback to help you determine how to prepare your students for standardized tests. In addition, you may become more sensitive to the needs of parents as they attempt to understand this area.

TWO TEACHERS' VIEWS

Karen was hard at work correcting her first-graders' practice tests when Sharie, another first-grade teacher, entered the faculty room and took a seat next to her. "I can't believe you are spending more time on those practice tests," challenged Sharie. "How much time are you going to spend on this before you decide your kids are ready?"

"I don't think my kids will ever be ready," replied Karen. "It seems like the more they do, the more careless they get. Look at Jason's test. He skipped at least three questions. If I've told him once, I've told him a hundred times, don't leave unanswered questions, and be sure to check your work!"

"If you want my opinion, I really don't think you are helping your kids at all," retorted Sharie. "All you are doing is getting them and yourself upset about this ridiculous test. I think you would be a lot better off just letting it happen. That's why I don't bother with any of this pretest nonsense. I'd rather just use the class time for regular reading groups, and whatever happens on the test, happens. They usually do O.K. on the test, anyway."

"How can you say that when two of your kids almost got knocked out of the second-grade book because they did so poorly on the test at the end of last year? Don't you remember the hassle you had last year with their parents and our fearless leader Frank on this? It took you a week to straighten it out with the reading supervisor. There's too much at stake to just ignore these tests," said Karen. She continued forcefully: "I send notes home a week before the test to remind the parents to have the kids get a good night's sleep the night before the test and to eat a good breakfast. I want my parents to know how important these tests are. Last year Mike Madison's mother even took the morning off work so she could get him up, feed him breakfast, and personally deliver him to my classroom door. She told me that she was probably more nervous than Mike."

"Well, to each his own," remarked Sharie flippantly as she left the faculty room and headed for the playground.

CHILDREN'S PERCEPTIONS: STANDARDIZED TEST TIME

It's obvious from this faculty room exchange that first-grade teachers can and do have different perspectives on standardized testing. It is also well known that standardized test results are of no small import to school district personnel. Interviews with school district administrators bore this out.

Less obvious, however, and sometimes not even considered, is the way children view standardized reading tests and how classroom practices and teacher attitudes toward testing color children's perceptions of reading. My research with first-graders revealed that standardized tests heavily influenced their overall perceptions of reading. Numerous first-graders alluded to test-taking when asked about what reading meant to them. I decided to explore this issue further, so I conducted interviews with twenty-five first-grade children shortly after they had taken their standardized reading tests in May.

In an attempt to see if they voluntarily offered any information about the test, I began each interview by asking, "What did you do in school today?" All twenty-five of the children referred to the testing activity. However, some said, they "took a test," while others indicated that they "had to do a booklet filled with work." Two children from the same class explained that they "did special seatwork but had to take our time."

Their descriptions of the test-taking activity were quite elaborate. Joseph explained:

I took a test today. I had to read way too many stories and answer questions. The hardest part was filling in a little circle that was the right answer. I kept getting mixed up, and I think I knew some answers but probably filled in the wrong one.

Most of the first-graders described reading stories and answering questions quite briefly. The majority, however, were either engrossed in the details of the answer forms or confused by them. First-graders indicated in most cases that using the forms was often more difficult than figuring out the correct answer. Tina said, "I didn't have time to do all the stories. I did 'em fast. But it took me a long time to find which circle to do." Raymond boasted:

It took me so long to fill in the whole circle. You can't have any white, then it's wrong. I know I got some questions wrong because Mrs. Siebert took the book and I had lots of questions to do. I filled the circles in so good. You couldn't see any white.

Kyle exclaimed:

Today we took a test about filling in these little circles and reading different sentences. It was kind of hard 'cuz you had to fill in little circles and stuff. It was so boring. All the circles had to be filled and no white could show. I lost my place once, but I still filled in all the circles. So I might have gotten those wrong.

An opportunity exists to shed further light on test results by once again listening to children. Perhaps a discussion following the testing would provide teachers with additional information beyond mere test scores. Kyle's comment about losing his place may call into question the accuracy of his test score. Kyle may indeed be able to read at a level well above what the test was able to measure.

Their understandings, however, went beyond mere descriptions of the test-taking task. A number of students thought, possibly correctly, that the test was given to see what reading group they would be placed in. One first-grader commented, "I am in the high group and if I did good on the test I'll be in the high group again in second." Another said, "Everyone has to take the test to see what reading group to be in." Keith exclaimed, "If you do good on the test, you'll be in a high reading group. If you do bad, you go in a low group. If you do really bad, the teacher said you go to special reading for help."

Other students thought the test determined whether you passed or failed the grade. As one first-grader articulated, "I'm glad we had lots of practice tests until they were all done. We practiced for the test. If you fail 'em, you fail for the whole year." Another first-grader indicated, "The test we took tells the teacher and our parents if we go to second grade." One student seemed rather puzzled when she said, "I wonder if this goes on your report card to see if you get held back?"

Still other children thought the tests were given to help them. Joey said, "You take these tests so the teacher can see what you need help in. You can't fail or anything. But you need to help the teacher see what to teach you next year." One first-grader really tried to help me understand what these tests were all about:

Everyone has to take these tests. They're called standardized. Even the kids that can't read take them. That way the teacher next year knows if you can read. It helps kids so they don't have to learn work over again the next year.

Another first grader indicated that, "The tests help you know what words you have to study before you get to second grade."

Preparation for taking standardized tests was also a major factor in how first graders thought about this experience. They frequently talked about what their parents and teachers told them to do to "get ready." Some children appeared to undergo little preparation. Eric said, "My teacher wrote my parents a note telling them we were having a test tomorrow. I forgot I had to take it until my mom reminded me. Stephen [Eric's friend] practiced the test in school. We didn't have to."

Many students, however, commented on the amount of time spent or at least the fact that time was spent practicing sample tests to get ready for the end-of-year standardized testing. Mary Anne commented, "I am glad we took the test today. Now we won't have to take those practice tests anymore." Another child said:

> *We had to do practice tests during science time for so long. I hate it 'cuz science is my best subject. I'm glad the test is over 'cuz we left off with rocks and minerals. Now I can bring in my collection for science. I have over about a hundred rocks to bring in for science.*

Another student, Roxie, claimed, "We have been practicing answering the questions and filling in the circles during math group, and now we will go back to our math groups."

The time for practicing for standardized test-taking has to come from somewhere; and many students, as these quotations illustrate, indicated that it came from time that had been allocated for content area subjects. Even more ironic, sometimes reading itself goes by the wayside to make way for test practice. Cindy explained:

> *Our teacher used to read us the Polk Street books after playtime every-day, but we had to stop to practice. Now we will be finishing Book Four because we won't have to practice any more. We had to put the book away until the test was over. Now we get to read Book Four.*

Heather, another first-grader, said, "We have been practicing for the tests for the whole year. Everyone will pass them because we've been learning these since the beginning of the year."

These first graders' understandings and observations of standardized testing, like other perceptions of reading, can be linked with instructional practices used in the classroom. As the scenario presented in the beginning of this chapter illustrates, teachers often approach standardized testing from various perspectives. Interviews with first-grade teachers support this notion. When discussing standardized tests, one rather utilitarian teacher stated:

> *Let's face it, these tests matter, for me and for the kids. Everyone looks at the tests and makes judgments about whether I have been successful in teaching, and we use these scores when the kids go into reading groups*

in September. I'm up front with the kids. I tell them they are important and they have to do well. Their best. I owe it to them.

At the other end of the continuum, a first-grade teacher exclaimed:

First-graders do not need to experience the pressure of tests. I tell my students that they are going to have "special seatwork," and that's as far as I'm willing to go. I can't believe some teachers actually take up valuable time to practice filling in circles with number two pencils.

A more moderate position was taken by Emily, another first-grade teacher, who said the following about standardized testing:

Some teachers go totally off the wall with these things. That doesn't do them or the kids any good. Some practice for months or weeks, and, by the time the tests are given, the kids' scores are either artificially inflated—this will catch up with them next year—or they freak out under the pressure and blow the test. Me, I prefer a more balanced approach. I explain what the tests are about, a week in advance, and then I give them a few practice lessons to make sure they are familiar with the format. The day of the test, I keep things relaxed but kind of businesslike. I definitely want them to do their best, but a good score is only worth so much practice time. Besides, I don't want to turn in inflated scores because that will only hurt them in second grade. Actually, one of my biggest challenges is to keep the parents calm and give them the proper information about the tests. Many of them start talking standardized tests and reading groups from day one. Some put way too much pressure on their kids to do well. Sometimes I wonder where this whole measurement thing came from.

These examples of classroom practices enable us to begin to link classroom practices with children's understandings of what standardized tests are all about. In fact, a very direct connection can be made.

In most cases the first-graders in the classes that practiced filling in circles for months or weeks in advance of the test typically viewed standardized tests as paper-and-pencil tasks with instructions like "Fill in the whole circle" and "Be careful not to go outside the lines." Many of those children had perceptions that were dominated by the task itself. Children in classrooms where teachers urged, "Do your best so you can stay or move into a high reading group," typically had understandings of standardized tests that included group placement and/or advancement. Children who received no admonition or direction from their teachers seemed to be rather oblivious to the tests and simply viewed them as "extra seatwork" or "workbooks to work in." First-graders' perceptions of standardized tests, like other perceptions discussed, are heavily influenced by classroom practices. Again, as teachers, we must remember that there is a direct link between the way we think about and prepare children for standardized reading tests and their understanding, and we should adjust our instruction accordingly.

PARENTS' ROLE

The home also plays a role in the standardized testing scenario. Sandy told me, "My teacher said, 'Now, on Sunday night you must have a good night's sleep and a good breakfast in the morning.' " Another child, Larry, remarked, "My teacher is very worried about this test. She said the whole class needs to get a very good night's sleep so we can do our best in the morning." These statements ("Eat a good breakfast," "Get a good night's sleep," "Make sure you are well rested") were all typical comments directed to home preparation that first-graders heard from their teachers.

Many students indicated that their parents received letters from the school communicating the importance of the tests. In most cases, this is how the parents got involved in helping their children "get ready" for standardized test day. The following letter is typical of the numerous examples I examined in my research.

Dear Parents:

Next week we will be administering the Iowa Tests of Basic Skills to students in grades one through six. The test is designed to measure growth in fundamental skills such as vocabulary, reading, and mathematics. You will receive a profile sheet indicating how your child has done on this test. On the profile sheet you will be given the local and national percentiles.

As with any testing situation, it is important that your child be well-prepared. In order to be well-prepared, please make every effort to ensure that your child has an adequate night's sleep, the proper nutrition, and is in attendance. Your child should have a good eraser and two #2 pencils (soft-lead) since the test is machine scored.

If you have any questions regarding this test, please contact me at school.

Sincerely,

Patricia Kane
Principal

Many children talked about the specific ways in which their parents helped them get ready for the tests. One child remarked that his father gave the following advice before he left for school: "Do good on your test. Concentrate. Most of all, don't be nervous." Many children indicated that their parents made them go to bed earlier than normal and eat a good breakfast because the teacher had directed the parents to do so.

In many cases, according to the first-graders interviewed, the early-to-bed and good-breakfast directives were enforced by the parents. In one situation, however, a parent commented when she dropped her son off at school, "I couldn't believe it! He actually put himself to bed last night and reminded me to make sunny-side-up eggs. I don't think I've cooked them in his life." This concern on the child's part was also suggested when another parent came to pick up her son. "He woke up at 6:00. He never wakes up on his own. Well, so much for a good night's sleep. I'm not so certain he wasn't anxious."

In many cases the parents' role seemed to go far beyond monitoring the child's eating and sleeping, as some parents clearly took on a more active role in the standardized test-taking process. Many parents made comments to the classroom teacher or to me about testing, and I often followed up with a phone call asking if they would mind elaborating on their comments.

Several parents suggested that there is a great deal of communication among parents to better understand the results of the tests and how their children did in comparison to friends and relatives. One mother indicated, "I had one friend call quite upset to see why or how her son could have gone from the 90th to the 50th percentile." Another parent said:

> I had this one friend, the father of a second-grader, tell me that his child was reading at a fifth-grade level because he got a 5.2 on the Iowa. I had to explain that he wasn't necessarily at a fifth-grade level, and he was really disappointed. My sister is a teacher, and she explained how that worked. I can see how he thought that. He was ready to buy new books that would have been super hard.

One father declared:

> I checked to see how my brother-in-law's kids did on their test, and John had them beat by at least twenty points. He should do better. He always gets higher grades on report cards. I'm not too worried. He does fine on these tests.

Another mother was puzzled by the percentile scores and told me that she called a neighbor when the scores came in the mail:

> She's a speech teacher and knows how to figure these things out. I guess my daughter is right in the middle. Doing average. Right at fifty. My

sister's kids were in the seventies and up. I was surprised they did that much better. My daughter reads way more than my sister's kids. My neighbor said that some are just better test-takers than others.

Another parent said:

When I got the test scores in the mail I really couldn't figure them out. I called a neighbor who was good with numbers and she told me what everything meant. My son is reading three years above where he should. He's in first grade and reading at fourth grade. I was thrilled. I found out her son is learning disabled and is way below in school.

Although it appears that many of the parents became involved in both the preparation for tests and the analysis of scores, it is important to note that I am reporting what was volunteered by some parents. Many parents did not become involved in this process at all, and when I spoke to some children they indicated that their parents did not mention anything about the test. It would be misleading to paint the picture of all the first-graders getting bedtime hugs, being put to bed early, and having sunny-side-up eggs for breakfast, and all parents calling one another with great interest about what these scores mean. As one first-grader said, "We didn't talk about the test last night. I gave my mother the note. My teacher read it to us. We didn't do things different." Another first-grader said, "I was at my aunt's birthday last night 'til 11:00. I almost didn't come to school today but remembered we had them reading tests." One of the first-graders reluctantly told his teacher, "My mom lost the note so I didn't get to bed early."

In most cases, children of parents who viewed high test scores as a status symbol typically viewed standardized tests in the same way. Parents who viewed the tests as determinants of whether their children pass or fail, in many cases passed that anxiety to their first-graders. And, of course, parents who put the test in a context of back to school–like drama and anticipation were more likely to get the same sleepless night, waiting, instead of the good night's sleep that everyone had hoped for. Parents might be advised through the school that their behavior appears to influence how their children view standardized test situations as well as reading in general. Parents also need a better understanding of what these tests are designed to measure, how to interpret the results, and how to prepare their children appropriately.

School personnel should recognize that they influence greatly how parents think about standardized testing. A note sent home announcing the test might accurately explain the purpose for the tests and how parents can best prepare their child, or it might be an anxiety-producing threat that can be counterproductive to the goals and objectives of the testing program. To alleviate confusion, parent conferences, a "teaching about tests night" or "test information night" or perhaps a handbook might be developed to help the parents understand what the tests measure and how to communicate with their children to prepare them for the tests. Most important, teachers might want to talk to parents about the complexity of the situation and assure them that there is no one "perfect" way for parents to act, or one "perfect" thing to say to all children. Through their communications, teachers can help parents avoid putting undue pressure on their children, making them feel that if they don't do well their parents will be disappointed or angry. Similarly, they can help parents avoid the pitfall of going to the other extreme, choosing to say nothing about the tests, which may not be helpful for those students who need information or reassurance. Perhaps the best advice teachers can pass along is to listen to children as they approach the time of testing. Just as listening is important for teachers, it is critical for parents as well. Since each child is unique, it is important for parents to listen and take cues from their own children in order to determine how much attention should be given to the anticipated tests.

One need only enter the halls of an elementary building at the end of the school year to appreciate the seriousness of standardized testing. Silence fills the hallways, and doors are closed with signs posted: "TESTING: DO NOT DISTURB." Students and teachers are cloistered in the confines of their own classrooms, with not a soul or a sound to be heard anywhere.

There has been much controversy lately regarding the appropriateness of standardized tests in our schools, especially at the primary grade levels. Although the use of standardized tests is still very much a part of our current educational system, and a multimillion-dollar industry has been advanced to support it, it is being challenged in many states and by many school districts. With the advent of whole language, assessment has taken on new dimensions. Yetta Goodman (1977) coined the phrase "kid watching" to characterize informal observation. She suggests that a great deal of information can be learned as teachers observe children during daily classroom activities. Others have concluded that there should be dramatic changes to improve the ways we currently evaluate reading (Johnston, 1992; Pikulski, 1989; Taylor, 1990). Johnston suggests that the "best option we have is to seek low-test solutions to as many of the problems of schooling as we can, and thus to render most testing blatantly wasteful if not obviously destructive. At the same time, we must set the conditions for the community to begin to see the limitations, and the unfortunate consequences of testing" (pp. 349-350). Pikulski's summary of recommended changes includes a significant decrease in the way teachers and administrators rely on standardized tests, while Taylor urges us to explore the use of biographic accounts of children's literacy behaviors.

Although most schools continue to use traditional methods of evaluation such as standardized testing, some are replacing or supplementing these formal approaches. Currently, evaluation tools such as observation, checklists, anecdotal records, and portfolios are considered by some as viable ways to chronicle children's growth and development. Children are also being encouraged to monitor their own reading progress through the use of journals, as they reflect on their reading interests and behavior.

I have purposely not focused on whether standardized tests are good or bad, overused or started too early, because those are not the issues that the children talked about. Many voices, including those of teachers, are being heard in regard to these issues. Although many are reacting to the shortcomings and misuses of standardized tests, most teachers at present do not have a choice about administering tests to students.

Through the children's comments about testing, I have come to understand the importance of teachers helping parents communicate with their children, providing limited practice opportunities to familiarize children with the test-taking routine rather than "teaching to the test," explaining honest purposes for giving the tests, and informing children that test-taking and reading are not the same processes.

Jeanne Reardon (1990), in "Putting Reading Tests in Their Place," describes how she has successfully taught "reading-test" reading as a separate genre to prepare students for taking formal tests. She claims that the tests are of little use, but acknowledges their importance in that they are used to make critical decisions about her students and the reading program. Reardon describes how she sensibly integrates "reading-test" reading into her instructional program in a manner that does not compromise the quality of reading instruction that goes on in her classroom. After a general discussion about a variety of kinds of reading children had done one day, Reardon passed out the first page of the practice items for the reading test along with pencils. "I told the children to read the page and write down anything they noticed—then we would talk about this new kind of reading." The practice page contained the following items taken from a Criterion Referenced Reading Test (Montgomery County Public Schools, 1987, p. 1):

1. Read the story.
   Think about who is sad.

"Mrs. Cook," said Maggie.
"I want to be in the school play."
"The play is for big boys and girls," said Mrs. Cook.

"I see," said Maggie.
She looked down.
"Big girls like Ellen."

Maggie walked out of the room.

Who is sad?

    A. Ellen
    B. Mrs. Cook
    C. Maggie

2. Read the story.
   Think about what is wrong.

"Didn't you buy the cookie jar?"
Tom's mother asked.

"I sure did," said Tom.
"The same one that was in the paper.
It's a happy cookie jar, Mom.
Because it has a smile.
Grandma and Grandpa will like it."

"Where is it?" asked Mother.
"What did you do with the bag?"

Tom looked down and all around.
"Oh no!" he cried.

What is wrong?
  A. Tom can't find his Grandma in the store.
  B. Tom can't find the cookie jar he bought.
  C. Tom can't find the bag his mother is looking for.

After reading the practice items, Reardon's students had much to share about this new genre:

Child 1: It's not a story.

Child 2: What do you mean?

Child 1: It doesn't explain. Like, you can't figure out why...

Child 3: It doesn't tell enough. You don't know anything about Maggie, and who's Ellen?

Child 4: Who is Mrs. Cook? There's Mrs. Cook and Tom and his mother and Maggie and...

Child 5: No. Tom and his mother are another story. There's two stories on this paper.

Child 6: It'd be better if there was pictures. And it was longer.

Child 7: Like a real story. Alex's right. It's not a story. It's too short. It's, it's, it's not anything.

Child 8: It's hard to read. I don't like it. It's dumb.

Child 9: You know, it's funny. It's not very long, and it took me a long time to read and figure out. I couldn't tell what was going on. I had to read it over and over and I still don't know. I don't get Maggie. Why does she say "I see"?…and it seems like she'd want to know why she can't be in the play. The first time I read it I thought she asked, "Big girl like Ellen?"—like it was a question. It's really confusing. Is it supposed to be?… And I don't get what it means when it says, "What is wrong?"—wrong? I just don't get it.

Child 10: It can't be a story 'cause stories don't have questions at the end.

Child 11: Some books have questions. I read a book about animals that was all questions and answers. So you can have books like that.

Child 10: Yeah, but those are questions for real answers. They, like tell you what you want to know. This's got A, B, C, for answers. They're dumb answers. You gotta guess. It doesn't tell you anything.

Child 12: The answers are tricky. Do you get one or two answers for the cookie jar one? I think Tom left the cookie jar at the store…so he can't find the cookie jar and he can't find the bag.

Child 13: It's very strange. It looks funny…it doesn't look like other reading. I make words dark and big when I want the reader to stop and notice, or be scared, or 'cause it's loud, or something like that…Who wrote this?… It goes up and down like newspapers, but it's not like a newspaper. It tells you what to do. It doesn't let you find out for yourself. (pp. 33–34)*

Reardon, a first-grade teacher, shows us how the children in her class were able to uncover many important characteristics of the reading-test form of writing as they compared it to more familiar genres. Reardon helps her first-graders take control of the testing situation over four days, during their twenty-minute reading time, by reading the practice test in between their self-selected books with "friends, helping, talking, and debating just as they do when reading real literature" (p. 36). She concludes, "I cannot ignore reading tests, nor can I allow them to control my classroom. 'Putting reading tests in their place' is the alternative I use while we search for a form of assessment worthy of the classroom literary community" (p. 37).

The enormous amount of time and energy some teachers spend to prepare their students for standardized tests is largely due to accountability. Standardized tests and other accountability requirements often put pressure on teachers to do things that teachers intuitively know are counterproductive. Reardon seems to have found a balance. She familiarizes her students with reading-test reading without letting standardized tests take over curriculum or pedagogy.

---

*The material on pages 103–105 is reproduced with permission from "Putting Reading Tests in Their Place" by S. Jeanne Reardon, *The New Advocate*, Vol. 3, No. 1, Winter 1990.

Perhaps we could also benefit from a lesson I learned from one of my students while teaching first grade. Mary was clearly the brightest student I had ever had in class. She could read literature typical of middle grades and was bored by division and fractions. Mary always said what was on her mind and often, without meaning to, offended her elders by her directness. But she was always honest and demonstrated insight well beyond her years.

I had just passed out all the standardized test booklets when Mary caught my eye and motioned me to come over to her desk. She looked me straight in the eye and said, "*You* know I know all this, and *I* know I know all this, so why are you wasting my time?"

Mary was right on one count, and for a moment I was speechless. Mary, however, for all her honesty and insight, did not understand the realities of the system. I explained to the child that neither of us had a choice; I had to give the test, and she in turn had to take the test. Mary gained a little wisdom that day, and I, a beginning teacher, lost a little idealism.

Mary's words have always helped me keep perspective, and have influenced my decision making regarding standardized testing. The first-graders in this study confirmed that their perceptions of standardized tests and the way we prepare for them affect children in ways that we cannot ignore.

A Classroom Teacher Responds...

If standardized tests were completely abolished from the primary grades, I would sleep better at night. However, these tests are a reality, at least for the present, and they must be dealt with on a professional level. As educators, we must come to terms with what these tests can tell us about our children and what the results will be used for.

Although teachers in some schools have a voice in terms of which tests are used, they have no control over the content of standardized reading tests. As teachers, however, we certainly can control the preparation and environment surrounding the test-taking situation. The children expressed concern over filling in bubbles on the answer key correctly, over having a great or not so great breakfast, and over the loss of valuable class time for things they wanted to do such as math or story time.

Have we created environmental settings during test time that are so different from the norm that neither the children nor the teachers function effectively? It seems that extremes at either end are not helpful. The overanxious teacher or parent creates an atmosphere that does not allow children to put forth their best effort; instead, the children may be driven to a highly anxious state because they know bathroom privileges are "on hold" until after the test, or a child falls asleep during the test because his big nutritious breakfast was more than his little body could handle.

The other extreme, whereby the teacher or parent says, "It's just another day," can also create an atmosphere that is not conducive to effective or accurate evaluation. Interruptions, discipline problems, or lack of materials simply compound the frustration of dealing with an unexpected, unexplained task.

What children really need is honesty—honesty on test-taking day and throughout the year. Teachers know what types of skills will be tested. These skills, if they correspond to the objectives set for the child and/or the grade level in general, will be taught throughout the year in the context of meaningful texts. We don't have to create a sterile, frightening environment just because the "directions" say to do so.

Not only do children need honesty; so do parents. I think we owe the parents of our schoolchildren an up-front, realistic look at what standardized test results show and what they do not show. We need to explain how the results are used and how to interpret basic scores. This information might be provided at a parent conference; or, if this is not possible, a letter could be sent home. It is fine to encourage parents to provide "ideal" conditions during testing times, but we have to be careful that we don't blow things out of proportion so that parents and children become more nervous instead of less.

Parents Respond...

Just as children instinctively know where they stand in comparison with one another, the desire of parents, teachers, school administrators, and government to know how kids "measure up" has driven our society to the use of standardized tests. Being tested periodically is a fact of life. Our children might as well get used to it early on.

Many parents want their children to be star performers, to be the best and the brightest. Parents hope doing well in school will give their children a good foundation for success in the adult world. Also, at least subconsciously, some parents see their children's successes as a measure of their own success. Thus, it's no surprise that parents want their children to do well on standardized tests at school and want to do whatever they can to help improve their children's performance at test time.

Parents can find the first few times a child is exposed to standardized tests confusing, as we did. What are the objectives of the test? How important are they? What should we do to help our child get ready? What do the results—with all those quartiles and percentiles—mean? Teachers and school administrators can save themselves a lot of headaches and help ensure that parents play a constructive role in the testing process with a well thought out pre- and posttesting communications program for parents. Parent–teacher meetings, parent–teacher conferences, and letters sent home with students all provide valuable opportunities to convey information about standardized testing.

Our school district always has positioned standardized tests as a necessary evil to meet state requirements. They are considered no big deal in the elementary grades. We have never heard any of our children talking about standardized tests in advance. Our children's first-grade teachers frequently pointed out that they use many means to assess pupil performance. They gave us extensive feedback at regularly scheduled parent–teacher conferences, via report cards, and by encouraging us to sit in occasionally on classroom instruction. In our school, second-grade placement of individual students is based on input from and talk among the principal, the various teachers who have worked with the pupil during first grade (the classroom teacher as well as art, music, and gym teachers and the librarian) and prospective second-grade teachers. The teachers have informed us that second-grade placement takes into consideration academic performance, maturity, and other factors. Prior to the time for standardized tests, a letter is sent to parents outlining what they can do to help their child get ready. After test results are available, our parent–teacher group sponsors a meeting where the administration reviews how results should be interpreted and answers questions parents may have.

After reading this chapter, we believe our district is handling standardized tests appropriately. Student performance should be assessed continually in all kinds of ways, formal and informal, so that classroom instruction can be adapted effectively to meet student needs. If teachers spend too much time preparing kids for standardized tests, they're shortchanging children's opportunities to do what they are in school for—to learn—in an already crowded school year. Some review of the mechanics of standardized tests, however, is appropriate (e.g., how to deal with all those circles!).

▶ 8

Home: The Beginning

PREVIEW

Children's understandings of reading are heavily influenced by their home environment. This chapter will enable you to see the dramatic influence of the home on early literacy. You will see the positive side of reading with children at home and the negatives that can be associated with parents attempting to act as teachers of unfinished work.

After reading this chapter, you may want to search for ways to connect children's out-of-school literacy experiences to the classroom. You also will want to be careful not to overburden parents and children with potentially inappropriate home reading experiences. Rather, you may choose to encourage first-graders and parents to continue to read together for pleasure as they have done in the past.

DOING HOMEWORK

Jana impatiently reached across the table and grabbed the pencil from her first-grade daughter's hand. "Here, let me show you how to do it." She took the pencil and forcefully drew lines between the pictures and the words on the ditto sheet. "Now let's see you do the next one on your own, Michelle. I'll watch, and you do it," she said tersely. Teary-eyed Michelle reached for the pencil with her hand, which was just beginning to tremble. She clearly was not enjoying this interaction with her mother. She stared at the paper intently, or at least pretended to. Michelle tentatively drew a line from a picture of a bicycle to the word *bicycle*, half looked up at her mother, and quickly dropped her eyes to the next picture on the page. After twenty long, tedious minutes, the paper was finally completed. Jana sighed, took the paper from Michelle, and quickly skimmed it for errors. Seeing none, she told Michelle that it was time to take a bath and get ready for bed. Michelle quickly slid from her chair, and on her way to her bath, turned toward her Mother, making eye contact for the first time in forty-five minutes, and asked, "Mommy, can we read a story tonight?" Jana sighed, and said, "Not tonight, Honey. I'm just too tired, and it's late." Michelle, having heard that response many times before, walked quietly away.

The frustration of doing worksheets and homework every night with Michelle had finally driven Jana to a breaking point. Not knowing what else to do, Jana dialed her sister Cynde and began to vent her frustration. "I just don't know what to do. Michelle and I are at each other's throat every single night. She doesn't even try anymore, and frankly, neither do I. It used to be so different when she was in kindergarten. We had fun then. The two of us used to curl up on the bed together almost every night, and I read to her. It felt so good to both of us. I just don't know why it has to be such a hassle now. Half the time I don't even know what she is supposed to do with the work she brings home, and neither does she. If it's like this in first grade, what's it going to be like later?"

Jana's sister, who had already had two children progress through grade 1, listened sympathetically and said, "Don't worry, Jana, Michelle will pick it up soon enough. The first-graders have to get through so much material. After she learns her letter sounds she'll be fine. There's probably nothing wrong. It's just going to take some time for her to learn her letters and read all the first-grade reading books." Jana seemed somewhat comforted by her sister, but she could not help longing for the days when she had felt comfortable just reading to Michelle.

HOME: WHERE CHILDREN LEARN TO READ

Most children's initial exposure to reading occurs at home. Homes as well as schools play an important role in children's perceptions of reading. In fact, many children feel that the home is where they have actually learned to read. In my study, time after time, first-graders remarked on how they were taught to read by a sister or an older brother, or just by "reading books with my parents."

The home emerged as such an important component of first-graders' perceptions of reading that I decided to examine these perceptions further. Interviews with parents of first-graders support the linkage between home reading activities and actually learning to read. As one mother remarked, "We used to sit for hours and hours looking at pictures and reading to one another. You know, she got so she could recognize a lot of the words in her book on her own." Another recalled how her daughter played school for hours on end:

> *Becca was always the teacher because she was two years older and in second grade. Steve was the student because he was the younger and couldn't read yet. After awhile that little guy began to catch on. Becca actually taught him to write his name, and somehow he memorized most of the stories in his books. It came so easily. I thought he would be terrific in school. I'm shocked that he is having problems.*

One parent talked about "rocking her baby and singing to her" after reading in a magazine that this was a verbal activity that would make her daughter a better reader. The parent commented, "I talked to her constantly when we went for walks, and read to her, without fail, every night. After awhile, long before school, Heather could read many words." Another parent commented:

> *I read to her a lot. We worked on letters and things like that. We spent a lot of time looking at books in the library, and "Sesame Street" was a*

ritual. It was so much fun for both of us. It was a special time we shared together. Erin actually read quite a few words before she ever got to school. Now she is busy teaching her little sister to read at home. The time goes by so quickly!

Children's perceptions were greatly influenced by these rich and usually pleasant encounters with reading at home. Most children enjoy the time spent when an adult or older sibling reads stories to them. As 7-year-old Tiffany remarked, "I like reading at home 'cuz me and my sister have a lot of books to read," or, as Mary said, "I love to sit on my Mommy or Daddy's lap and listen to a book. We love *Amelia Bedelia.* We always laugh."

For the most part, early reading at home was viewed positively by children and parents alike. Some children, however, indicated that there was little reading done at home. These comments were not usually generated as complaints but, rather, contrasted with someone reading to them elsewhere. As Michael said:

I like it when the teacher reads to us in school. She is reading a little bit of The New Kids at the Polk Street School *after lunch every day. It's my favorite thing. Oh yeah, playtime is better. I like reading time in school. My parents don't have time to read to me at home.*

Or, as Noel said, "I like reading in school. Nobody reads at home." Kristen indicated that she loved to go visit her Nana because, "She reads and reads and reads. It's nothing for her to read ten books. My mother never reads to me at home."

HOMEWORK: PARENT–CHILD CONFLICT

After children began formal reading instruction in school, reading seemed to take on a new and somewhat tense identity at home, as the expectations for both students and parents changed. Taylor (1983), in an ethnographic account of family literacy, described the first-grade experience as an "unsettling time," as well (p. 18). One of the more emotional and problematic reading-related experiences in the homes of first-graders seemed to center on homework, which often consisted of unfinished work and/or "reading" tasks not yet mastered.

First-grade teachers were very concerned with unfinished or incorrect reading work. Children got warnings, lost playtime, were denied stickers, and sometimes were denied promotion when reading performance was inadequate or work was incomplete. As one first-grade teacher said to me, "How can I possibly send him to second grade? He never finishes his work. Look at this workbook. Most of the pages are blank." Another teacher announced, "If your seatwork is not done, you will have to stay in during playtime. It's important that all of your workbook pages are done before play." Unfinished work and reading tasks not yet mastered become emotional issues in many classrooms, and the tension is often transferred to the home, thus creating problems for children and parents alike. It is important to recognize that these teachers made decisions such as sending work home with children and keeping them in from playtime in the best interest of the child in an effort to "prepare them for what was to come" (e.g., second-grade curriculum, standardized testing).

The negative feelings can be exacerbated by asking parents to solve this dilemma at home. Common first-grade practice is to send unfinished or unlearned work home for the first-graders and their parents to complete. The following examples of how two teachers approached homework illustrate this point:

Teacher #1

To be a good reader, you have to practice at home. We will be reviewing these words for quite a while. I will give you a list of those words you are having trouble learning and don't know, to take home and practice. Your parents can sign this sheet each day to show me you studied.

Teacher #2

Did you practice your words at home? You must study your words because you have forgotten some of them over the summer. It's your responsibility to study the words that give you trouble. Don't wait for your mom to take them out of your bookbag. Take your words out and show them to Mom when you get home.

The child being talked to immediately informed Teacher #2 that her mom isn't home when she gets home. The teacher then advised her to "show them to Mom when she does get home." First-grade teachers in this study clearly involved parents in a tutorial capacity.

This youngster raised a legitimate point when she indicated that there was no parent home to help her with her work when she came home from school. With most parents of school-age children working in this country, this is a common scenario that must be considered as teachers routinely send work home for parents to help their youngsters complete or master. As one parent I interviewed remarked:

I know I can help, but there must be a better way. By the time we get home from work, pick Chad up at the sitter's and eat, there's not much time left. I haven't seen him all day, and I just don't want it to be a struggle.

Or, as another parent lamented:

> *Even though we both have to work, we want to be part of Tina's education. It's important for parents to know what is going on in school and to help, but by the time we get home from work there's not a lot of time left. I don't want to fight with Tina when I haven't seen her all day, especially in first grade.*

Many parents of first-graders experience a great deal of frustration when they are cast in the role of teacher of unlearned lessons or taskmasters to children who have not completed their assignments. As one mother remarked:

> *To be honest with you, having a child in first grade is very frustrating. I understand the teacher has a great deal to cover, but I feel like Ryan is going to high school, not first grade. He is not adjusting to all of the homework he has at night. All we seem to do as a family is argue over homework that needs to be done. I have tried everything, but his dad and I have concluded that this is all too much for him. I thought he would be a good student since he is smart and all, but this homework thing has got us all bugged. I wish his teacher would just have him work hard at school and then play and do his activities at home. After all, this is only first grade.*

Another mother echoed the same sentiments when she remarked, "I can't believe the demands placed on such little kids. Do you know she has a good deal of homework every night?" A father seemed upset when he commented emphatically:

> *I want my kid to succeed, but every night we have to finish the papers that Joey didn't finish in school. He must have at least ten papers a day. It's just too much to ask. I wanted to have him join soccer, but now I don't know. Every night seems like a battle. But to tell you the truth, I don't blame him for wanting to play after being in school all day. He's just a kid.*

Many first-graders share their parents' feelings about after-school work and the frustration that goes with it. Eric commented, "I don't like reading at home anymore because my mom makes me read to her. She never reads to me anymore. She wants me to get better at reading." Or, as Jill remarked:

> *At the beginning of the year and when I was in kindergarten, my mom read to me every night. Now she says with my word lists and my other book we don't have time. I wish we could just read stories. I hate remembering my word lists.*

Not all parents of first-graders are as frustrated as those described earlier. However, most parents of first-grade children expressed a great deal of concern about how their children were doing in reading and were willing to figure out ways to help their children at home even though some view the demands as unreasonable for first grade. One father explained, "If this is what Ryan has to do to be successful in reading, that's what his mother and I will do. We may not agree with it, but we'll do what we must."

Other parents take an active role in their child's schooling with no complaints about what they are asked to do at home. As one parent said, "I don't wait to hear from the teacher; I call to see how Mary is doing." Another parent commented, "I love getting the note from Jennifer's teacher, with Jennifer's work, on Fridays. It lets us know exactly how she is doing. We know how many 'Excellents' she gets that week, and if she is having any trouble." Parents often made comments such as, "I had hoped Jane would be in the highest reading group." Or, as one father put it, "I am so worried that Terry won't read well. I want him to read better than I can. He can go any place if he learns to read and is a good reader." One teacher stated that parental concern was one of the highlights of teaching first grade. "I like teaching first grade because the parents are still so involved. They want to know how their children are doing, especially in reading."

As parents monitor their children's reading progress, they are often faced with difficult situations. One parent was reduced to tears when she talked about how her daughter was doing in reading:

> *The thing that is really bothering me is that the teacher told me that she is making a few of her letters backwards. Not all of the time, but some of the time. I thought this was normal in first grade. But she informed us that if it didn't stop by the end of the year, Heather would be retained this year. I felt like I was dreaming. Almost every paper has a star, and she is in the highest reading group. I didn't know kids could fail for something like that. When her homework is finished we work on those letters, like the teacher told us to, every night. I don't want her to fail this year. It wouldn't make any sense at all. The teacher was emphatic about this. I am really afraid we are putting too much pressure on her, but we are just so upset. I can't believe it is like this, and it's only first grade.*

Most educators would agree that Heather's reversals are being blown way out of proportion and hardly warrant this type of response from either the home or the school. Heather's teacher indicated to me during a later interview that she was certain that Heather would not fail first grade, as she was "a very smart little girl." She explained that she told the parents that Heather might be held back in order to let the parents know that they had a "responsibility to practice the letters at home with Heather." With little or no knowledge of visual discrimination, Heather's parents responded in the best way they knew. They drilled their daughter each night for months in hopes that this reversal problem would be corrected by the end of the year.

It became particularly troublesome in the first-grade reading scenario when parents were asked to function in a role similar to classroom teachers. Teachers frequently sent home incomplete work and lists of unmastered words and skills to be learned. Unfortunately, this was often the most difficult work that the child encountered in school, and untrained parents were often unable to help. This led to a great deal of frustration on the part of parents, as, prior to this, their reading role had been for the most part that of story reader, teller, and listener. Both parents and children were comfortable with this role, and the new expectations caused frustration for parents and children alike.

Fortunately, children's perceptions of reading at home seem to be uncolored by these difficulties reported by parents when the home is asked to be an extension of school. Children seem to disassociate homework with reading at home. Their understanding of reading at home has little connection to in-school activity. Although the work is done at home, first-graders consider this school reading. Parents, as mentioned, can become very frustrated with this situation, and this frustration dominates many first-grade parents' perceptions of first-grade reading instruction.

When the teachers in my study encountered these findings, they remarked without exception that they were unaware that sending unfinished and/or unlearned work home could result in this degree of frustration. They indicated that there appeared to be no good reason to continue the practice and, in light of the positive role that home can play, felt that the goals of the reading program would be best served by continuing the parent role of story reader, teller, and listener. They further commented that they would actually prefer not to send homework home with first-graders and, if given the choice, would elect to do much more child-centered reading during the school day. However, the teachers felt tremendous pressure to prepare the children for second grade and/or for standardized testing.

Simply eliminating homework will not solve this problem if teachers are accountable for completing an unrealistic minimum number of readers and workbooks during the school year; indeed, the teachers might feel even more pressure to do more during the school day if the homework component is eliminated! A reexamination of the entire system and curriculum may be in order. Patrick Shannon devotes the last chapter of his book, *Broken Promises*, to the "possibilities of constructive change," such as collective seminars where teachers would begin to analyze their dependence on basal reading programs and conduct actual research within their own classrooms. Shannon believes that, although it will not be easy, it is possible for teachers and students to gain control and resist the management of literacy in school and to "gain their rightful place in reading programs" (p. 147).

PARENTS: THE NATURAL ROLE

As parents discuss the role that reading plays at home, it is easy to recognize the contribution they make naturally in helping their children learn to read. It also helps us understand why children would be better served if parents continued their natural role as story reader, teller, and listener, and served as models when they read newspapers, books, and magazines, as these activities have served to sustain millions of youngsters' involvement in the world of reading. Jim Trelease (1990), author of *The New Read Aloud Handbook*, discusses the importance of reading aloud to children and offers valuable suggestions to teachers and parents to promote and implement reading aloud and reading for enjoyment at home as well as in the classroom.

According to the parents I interviewed, children were surrounded by print long before they entered school. Teale (1978) supports this notion and suggests that children's homes contain a variety of reading materials, including magazines, catalogs, books, reference material, and junk mail. Parents described reading to their children and talking to their children about print at home, in grocery stores, at restaurants, and on trips. Children in literacy-rich homes from a very early age participate in functional reading and writing experiences (Taylor, 1983), and storybook reading is often a daily routine (Durkin, 1966). Many parents interviewed in this study responded that they did not intentionally or systematically teach their children to read. In a study of children who learned to read before they entered school, Durkin (1966) found this, as well. The parents interviewed by Durkin claimed that no one taught their children to read. Upon direct questioning, however, many parents did answer questions such as, "What's that word?" but did not recognize this attention as teaching. John Holt discusses this in his book, *Learning All the Time* (1989), when he tells of the many parents who describe reading aloud to a child a favorite story, over and over again:

> One day they find that as they read the child is reading with them, or can read without them. The child has learned to read simply by seeing words and hearing them at the same time. Though children who learn this way probably couldn't answer questions about it, they have learned a great deal about phonics. Nobody taught them to read, and they weren't particularly trying to learn. They weren't listening to the story so that they would be able to read later, but because it was a good story and they liked sitting on a comfortable grown-up lap and hearing it read aloud. (p. 21)

One parent commented:

> *I just did what felt good. I loved reading stories, nursery rhymes and talking to Shannon as much as possible. We even read her the signs*

along the road. We weren't exactly sure how we were helping her, but knew it couldn't hurt. If she wasn't interested in what we were doing, we just stopped. After a while she knew how to read stop signs and recognized different products in the grocery store. By the time she got into kindergarten she recognized almost all of the signs that we would come across, even on a long trip.

Another parent echoed, "We spent a lot of time reading signs from the back seat of the car."

My study suggests that these activities greatly influence first-graders' perceptions of reading. As one first-grader explained, "It's important to read signs and stuff. I can read the word 'EXIT.' I know what it means, too." Another first-grader proudly claimed, "I can help my Dad drive when we go to Grandma's. I can read every sign—even 'DETOUR'!"

Many parents also expressed the importance of reading for fun. One parent explained:

I wanted to be sure Jimmy had good feelings about reading. I wanted him to know that reading can be exciting and a great joy. That's why I read to him every night. Maybe that's why now he'll pick up a book and just read.

Another parent echoed these remarks, "As far as I'm concerned, reading for little kids should just be fun." One parent described how relaxing reading was when her daughter was little. "I can remember reading to Elizabeth every night. She was just a baby, but I would rock her and read her a story. Most of the time she would just fall asleep. It was so relaxing."

Reading was also used to quiet children down after hard play. As one parent said, "When Sarah gets too excited, or off the wall, I read to her to help her relax." Another parent commented, "When I read to Doug it helps calm him down." Bedtime reading was perceived by parents to be a great transition from rough activities to passive activities, such as sleep. Parents reported that their children would often ask to be read to so they could "calm down."

First-graders talked a great deal about reading for fun and relaxation. As Chris stated, "Sometimes I read all by myself. That's fun and relaxing. I always do that every night. It makes me want to go to sleep." Another first-grader put it quite simply, "Reading is to have fun. I read at home every single night."

Parents indicated that, from their perspective, reading was more than just a source of fun and relaxation. They introduced or read books to their children as a source of knowledge or information. As one father explained:

Shawn got really into collecting rocks. We raided the library, and brought home all of the books we could find about rock collecting. We couldn't go outside without him using his book to identify the rocks he saw—based on descriptions and pictures in the books. Of course we encouraged this.

Another parent said, "When we got Karen the rabbit, we bought her a few books to read about taking care of pets. She looked at these books for hours." Other parents talked about reading books with their children about space, dinosaurs, shells, and a number of other topics, in order to help their children "read to learn."

Reading, as a source of knowledge or information, greatly influenced first-graders' perceptions of reading. As Casey said, "I read books to learn new things. It's fun to read because it's fun to learn." Karen discussed her interest in birds. "I have lots of books about birds. I read them and it helps me know all about the different kinds of birds that I see. I love birds. So does my grandmother."

As early as 1908, Huey recognized and wrote about the naturalness of learning to read at home:

> The child makes endless questionings about the names of things, as every mother knows. He is concerned also with the printed notices, sign, titles, visiting cards, etc., that come in his way, and should be told what these "say" when he makes inquiries. It is surprising how large a stock of printed or written words a child will gradually come to recognize in this way. (p. 314)

We must acknowledge the contribution of what parents do naturally in helping their children learn to read. Studies of beginning readers have consistently shown that early reading experiences, such as being read to, are crucial to children's reading development (Clay, 1979; Taylor, 1983; Teale, 1978). Reading acquisition might be best served by not forcing parents into the role of surrogate teacher but, instead, allowing them to continue their natural role— that of story reader, teller, and listener.

A Classroom Teacher Responds...

"Reading is fun," "Reading is relaxing," "Reading helps us learn," and "Learning to read is natural," should not simply be views that we would like to see continued at home, but they should also be views that we see as important for school.

I could easily relate to the teachers in the study who stated that they never realized that sending home incomplete work with first-graders could cause such a disturbance at home. Asking the parents for home support seems natural and sensible. Since becoming a parent of a first-grader, however, I am living through homework sessions of frustration, anger, and tears as I try to "help" my child complete work for the next day. I also clearly remember many nights of being too tired to read a bedtime story. I am not proud of these moments and really didn't think about the implications until reading this chapter.

More than ever before, I wholeheartedly understand the idea of having parents continue making their most valuable contribution to teaching our children to read—the daily oral reading or bedtime story. Even from the most skilled and patient parent, isolated skills activities will not develop a child's reading as much as a loving daily story. "Do what is natural and fun" is wonderful advice for all parents involved in helping their child learn to read.

As we continue to move into an age in education where schools, the community, and the family are being urged to work together, it makes sense that schools do more to promote the significance and appreciation of the parents' natural role as story reader, teller, and listener. Perhaps PTA meetings, school newsletters and parent conferences could be avenues to spread the word. The school might promote an evening workshop for parents where they could view and discuss a videotape of Jim Trelease, author of *The New Read Aloud Handbook* (1990). Parents might be invited into classrooms to "do what they do best," such as reading aloud a favorite story or talking to children about their real life experiences. Parents and teachers might work together to promote reading activities such as book fairs, read-a-thons, or PARP (Parents as Reading Partners). Finally, this chapter made me realize what rich literacy experiences children have in their homes and how much we can gain by listening and showing that we respect and value those experiences.

Parents Respond...

What a relief it is to us that the author concludes parents' role in helping children learn to read should be as story readers, story tellers, listeners, and example setters through reading themselves! This is what we do naturally. This feels right.

We have seen very little reading homework with our children in the first grade. Our children have brought home:

- Stories to read aloud to us, with a sign-off slip to be returned to the teacher, acknowledging completion
- Worksheets to be finished once every two or three weeks
- Weekly spelling lists to practice for Friday quizzes starting midyear

With none of our children have we ever sensed any homework-related tension, concern about keeping up, or concern about how they are doing—at least not in the first grade. We felt sorry for both the children and the parents as the author described their frustration over unfinished work.

Now that we think of it, there seems to be no logical sense in teachers' treating the home as an extension of the classroom for completing assignments and requiring parental involvement in that process. Parents cannot be in close enough communication with the teacher on a daily basis to provide seamless instruction or assistance. Most parents, whether they admit it or not, do not feel qualified to "teach" particular content matter, even at the first-grade level. Parents can be harried in the evening and all too often may fail to give nurturing assistance. In the evening, first-grade children are tired and do not have the attention span necessary to do serious work.

One issue that always concerns parents is television. The conventional wisdom is that television is detrimental to children's development as readers. Yet in the preschool years, "Sesame Street," "Mr. Rogers' Neighborhood," and other frequently watched programs may actually introduce beginning reading skills. As our children have entered school, we have tried to limit the time they spend in front of a television set so that they have more free time available for reading, playing, and communicating with us. In addition, we encourage our children to watch videotapes from our "library" rather than whatever happens to be on TV at a given moment. That way we can slant the material they view toward Walt Disney classics and other "good stuff." We try occasionally at bedtime to read the storybook version of a video they have watched during the day (e.g., *101 Dalmatians* or *Sleeping Beauty*) in an attempt to make that reading session more meaningful.

Parents generally want to do what they can to help their children succeed in school. With this in mind, it would be very beneficial for first-grade teachers to tell parents at the beginning of the school year what the parental role should be in the learning-to-read process and to suggest appropriate home activities, including some ideas for dealing with television. Ways to convey these messages might include letters sent home to parents, dialogue at school open house, or discussion at the initial parent–teacher conference.

▶ **9**

Siblings: Teachers and Learners

PREVIEW

In Chapter 8 you were exposed to the importance of the home in terms of early literacy development. Most of that chapter centered on parents and their first-grade children. In this chapter you will see that older siblings play a significant role in the reading development of their younger brothers and sisters. First-graders frequently credited older siblings with teaching them to read.

You may want to study and perhaps adopt some of the teaching strategies employed by older children as they teach younger children to read. You will particularly want to note the methods and materials used by the older "experts." Perhaps most important, you will become a wiser but humbler teacher after reading this chapter.

MELISSA TEACHES FRED TO READ

Melissa and Fred were curled up together under a blanket stretched between two chairs in Melissa's room. Four-year-old Fred sucked his thumb contentedly, his head resting on his 7-year-old sister's shoulder. Melissa was busy teaching Fred to read. Her technique was mainly one of reading aloud to Fred, with an occasional pause, at which time Melissa would point to the page and Fred would utter a word or phrase. Sometimes Melissa would tell Fred to sound a word out, and at other times she instructed him to guess. Most of the time, however, when Fred didn't know a word, Melissa would simply tell her brother what it was. After the first book was completed, it was Fred's turn to select a book that he would read for Melissa. He chose a very worn trade book that had obviously been read to him many times in the past. Putting on his best reading voice, he began to read one of his favorites, *Green Eggs and Ham,* by Dr. Seuss. "I am Sam. I am Sam. Sam I am..." Fred read without error. He did, however, turn the pages ahead of where the story line indicated he should be. It was clear that Fred had memorized the book from beginning to end. Melissa listened patiently, as Fred read on, page after page. She never once told him he was on the wrong page. When he finished reading, Melissa clapped, as she always did, and remarked, "Good, Freddy. You read it perfect again. Tomorrow we can do a new book."

OLDER SIBLINGS AS TEACHERS

This scenario is typical in that it presents Melissa, an older sibling, teaching Fred, a younger sibling, to read. Time after time, first-graders remarked that an older brother or sister had taught them to read at home. I decided, to interview these older siblings to understand better how they went about teaching their younger brothers and sisters to read. After all, according to the first-graders, the real instructional "experts" were their older brothers and sisters.

These first-graders were not talking about adult or even teenage siblings when they remarked that an older brother or sister had taught them to read. For the most part, they were referring to siblings two to four years older than they, siblings with whom they often played. Indeed, the siblings seemed to be more of a playmate than a tutor, teacher, or other authority figure. As 9-year-old Natalie remarked when asked who read with her younger first-grade brother, "Most often I do 'cuz my older sister is too busy and gets mad."

It should also be noted that the "teaching" generally seemed to span the preschool, kindergarten, and first-grade years. Many first-graders entered first grade with a wealth of reading experiences, compliments of their older brothers and sisters. Approximately equal numbers of girls and boys were identified as having been responsible for teaching a younger sibling to read. Similarly, approximately equal numbers of boys and girls indicated that they had been taught to read by an older sibling. Sex differences did not appear to be a factor in who was taught or who did the teaching.

I interviewed a total of thirty-one older siblings either at school or in their homes. The children interviewed were selected from a list of second- through fourth-graders known to have younger brothers or sisters in the first grade. The children were asked about "reading" with their younger siblings. When they indicated that, yes, they read with their younger siblings, they were asked to describe the types of activities they did when they read with, or attempted to teach, their younger brothers and sisters. They were also asked about where and when they taught the younger children.

Much of the early reading instruction occurred in one of the siblings' bedrooms or a bedroom shared by both children. When asked how they taught the younger children to read, the bedtime story was frequently identified by the second- through fourth-grade "experts" as a reading instructional activity. Comments like 9-year-old Brian's are common. "Well, I like to read to him because every night he can't go to sleep without a bedtime story, so sometimes I read to him."

But the bedtime reading scenario appeared to be more than just reading. Older siblings described bedtime reading activities that had heavy doses of love and caring as well. Nicole, a third-grader, made reading a warm, comfortable experience for her then preschool brother, John:

> *Yeah, when he was little, my mom or me would try to rock him to sleep. He used to sleep in my room. I was eight years old or something. He used to sleep in his crib and suck on his bottle, and I used to tell him, 'John-John want to hear a book?' 'Cuz that's the only way he'd go to sleep, to read a book. But I wouldn't read him a book. I'd make up my own story out of my mouth. 'Cuz I used to memorize them [stories]. I*

used to memorize them a lot. Three Little Pigs… Snow White…*things like that. I'd usually read some outta the book and make up half of the story, like the Good Witch, and I used to go, 'The Good Witch is gonna come and the Good Witch is gonna give ya a little teddy bear' or something, and he used to love that. He used to love witches, and I used to tell him all about them. He used to like the good ones, I mean. The bad ones he used to cry a little bit, but I never told him about the bad ones, so I used to rock him. I used to rock him to sleep with a book or something. Especially with the witches; he loved them.*

Has there ever been a warmer, more tender teacher of children? Can storytelling and story reading be more effectively integrated? Truly, the bedtime story setting is a vital early reading experience and has been identified as such by the individuals most often cited as having taught a first-grade child to read—the real experts, older brothers and sisters.

Taylor (1983), in an ethnographic study of family literacy, also found that older siblings play a role in their younger brothers' and sisters' reading development. She described an older sister propping her younger sister up "in her pumpkin seat when she was only six-months-old so that she could see the pictures as Kathy read her a story" and of a younger sibling "echoing his sister's words as she spoke" (p. 17).

If we recognize the legitimacy of older siblings as teachers and attempt to learn from them, then Nicole's remembrance of rocking her brother John-John to sleep with "a book or something" instructs us to make warmth, comfort, and yes, perhaps, love part and parcel of the early reading experience. Somehow, Nicole seemed to know how to combine them all. Fortunately for all of us, Nicole, perhaps through her own experiences, had the insight to recognize the importance of these bedtime reading experiences in John-John's early reading exposures and was able to articulate them perceptively.

Clearly, the bedtime story scenario was viewed as an important early reading experience by older siblings; it was mentioned repeatedly in over 90 percent of the interviews as an example of teaching younger siblings to read.

Not all instruction occurred in the bedroom, however, as older siblings mentioned a number of other instructional settings, including virtually every location in the house. Local libraries were also frequently mentioned. The "best" setting of all seems to be in a makeshift blanket and pillow fort made by the children, even if it is not always allowed by their parents. The bedroom, however, was by far the most frequently mentioned setting for instruction.

The bedtime story instruction, for the most part, is warm, gentle, and painless, but that is not always the case with other forms of teaching. Older brothers and sisters can be taskmasters at times.

As Jackie remarked about teaching her younger sister, Katie, to read:

Um, well, um, when we play school I usually give her workbooks and then make her draw, and then I show her the paper, and I tell her to read the directions to herself. If there's like a paragraph, I make her read it to herself and...I make her sound out the words, and if she can't sound it out, I'll tell her. And if she knows her paper and she can do it, I make her do it.

Jackie's view of teaching certainly had an authoritarian slant. She clearly felt that Katie must be "made" to perform these reading-related tasks, and, interestingly, she described the reading scenario as "playing school." One must wonder about the origin of her teaching role model.

On occasion, the instructional setting in the home proved quite disruptive, as Nick, age 9, described how he worked with his younger sister:

When she don't know a word, I tell her it, and when she says the wrong words, I tell her she said the wrong word! She says she didn't. I said she did, and we argue. She doesn't like to read, but I make her read. But she always shoots books around the room. She don't like a part, she shoots 'em. But I make her read because Dad, he likes listening to people read. And I go, "You better read that. Dad'll slap ya." And she goes, "No he won't" and kept on doing that.

Certainly Nick's approach is a bit extreme, and once again we must inquire as to his instructional (or disciplinary) role model.

The most popular materials used to teach younger siblings to read were found to be trade storybooks. Older siblings are readily able to list books they have used to teach their younger brothers and sisters to read. Moreover, they frequently have elaborate rationales for having selected a particular book to use with their younger sibling.

Older brothers and sisters were particularly sensitive to the difficulty level of the books they chose. Time after time, they remarked how they looked for books that were "easy to read" or something that their younger brother or sister could "handle," as this excerpt from an interview with 9-year-old Jackie demonstrates:

Yeah, I pick out lots of books for Katie. I pick out, like, Dr. Seuss books 'cuz she likes them a lot, and she can read them by herself. And that's one book that she can read, and it's funny, and she always reads that so I think it's nice to pick out that book for her. If she gets a hard book, I tell her, "Katie, go back and pick out an easier book." She usually tells me if they're hard or easy. Sometimes I just think they're hard or easy,

*'cuz I look at the words 'cuz she always reads words and some books
are hard 'cuz they have too many words and they're too hard to read.*

While Jackie was not exactly scientific in her assessment of a book's relative
readability, no one can argue with her sensitivity to her sister's need to read
books that are easy.

Nicole also demonstrated a sensitivity to the hard/easy issue and the
importance of supplying younger siblings with books they can read. When
asked if she ever picked out books for her younger brother in the library, she
replied:

*Yes I did. I picked up a few books that he likes. He usually reads kiddie
books, you know what I mean? Like stories about the Three Little Pigs, or
something. He likes those kinds. He's interested more in that, than big
stories. A big story has more words and stuff like that, and a kiddie
story is like, has little short words on every single page and stuff, and it
really doesn't need each word. There is more interest and stuff in kiddie
books. The big ones aren't that interesting. In the kiddie books, they
have more, better pages and more better stuff in it. The words are
shorter and easier to read. Something like that, you know? It's more for
them than for us, 'cuz we're out of that stuff. We used to read it, but
now we mostly know the words in it, and it would bore us, stuff like
that—it's sorta easy. And now in the thick books, they have more stuff
for us. Interesting stuff for us than they do for when we were in second
grade. Yeah, kiddie books have short words and pictures—pictures to
guess from when you don't know the word.*

Nicole's treatise on the differences between "kiddie books" and "thick
books" clearly demonstrates insight into the importance of readability and
interest level of the trade books. Her lesson to us seems to be to help beginning
readers choose materials they can easily handle.

Older siblings are not merely speaking of hard and easy, however, when
they talk about selecting books for their younger brothers and sisters. The
interest appeal of the book to the individual child is also heavily considered. As
9-year-old Missy related about selecting books with her 6-year-old brother
Jeffrey:

I read Mike Mulligan and the Steam Shovel *to Jeffrey, but I always let
him pick out the books he wants from the "Little Good Books for
Children" in his book club. I do this so I know they're the ones that he
likes. He likes building sort of stuff, like that, because he says he wants
to be a digger man when he grows up. So he likes building lots of times.*

Sometimes he looks for, like, funny stuff. When he gets new books, we read them to him a lot, and he always laughs. He has a funny little giggle, and um, he, the funny ones he laughs at, and he looks at the pictures and listens to the words, and sees the cover. So he just sees the cover and stuff, so he gets it. He finds out if it's funny. Sometimes, like if there's a book order, I show Mom what might be nice for Jeff. Something he might like. I tell her to get him the mechanical stuff and stuff like that. Sometimes I look for active stuff that he can do, like a pop-up book or something, 'cuz he likes those. And I got him a Clifford book, Clifford Wants a Cookie, *'cuz it came with cookie cutters, too. So we baked some cookies, and he helped me.*

It's clear that 9-year-old Missy had made some very insightful observations. She understood that her brother Jeffrey needed to be given an opportunity to choose his own materials, and, perhaps more important, she understood that Jeffrey was perfectly able to do so. After all, Jeffrey was able to "get it" (meaning) by looking at the pictures, listening to the words, and seeing the cover.

Missy also realized that her 6-year-old brother does well with active books, books that pop up or come with cookie cutters. She knows that when she chooses books for him, she should look for active books or at least books that are funny or are about building things. Clearly, she is sensitive to her younger brother's need to be actively involved with the books he is reading.

Assisting her mother with Jeffrey's selection was a further indication of her level of maturity and sophistication as a tutor/teacher. It was not clear whether her mother actually heeded Missy's input, but the selection would undoubtedly be appropriate if she had. This 9-year-old child is not at all casual about the book selection process, nor should we be.

Some of the siblings look beyond the length of the words, the cover, or the content. Greg was an 8-year-old who had discovered that his 6-year-old sister had a preference for specific authors:

I look at the man who's writing it. I mean, I read the man who's writing it. Like, Shel Silverstein. He writes in cursive. My little sister likes to read his books a lot.

Greg seemed to have identified another important characteristic of a book to assist him in the selection process. The book's author clearly was an important point to be considered by Greg as he thought about his sister's reading enjoyment.

The interviews conducted with the older siblings about teaching their younger brothers and sisters to read were rich with information about choosing books. In fact, almost one-third of the total content of the interviews with older siblings centered around selecting the "correct" book for each reader. Perhaps the older siblings' sensitivity to this issue is heightened as a result of their own young age (average age 7 years 8 months) and the fact that books are still being selected for them by others. Or it may be simply that children are more sensitive to other children's needs. It is also conceivable that older siblings have learned by trial and error that it is far better to read with their little brothers and sisters in materials they enjoy, rather than force them into materials that are not as enjoyable to read. Whatever the reason, there is clearly a lesson to be learned here, as selecting the "right" book for their younger brother or sister is a top priority for the older sibling.

The only area that received more attention than selection of reading materials in the interviews with older siblings was how they actually taught the younger children to read, or the actual reading instruction employed. Instruction was not left to chance, as each "expert" clearly had his or her own favorite method(s) of instruction.

Perhaps one of the most popular methods employed was the everyday sound-it-out approach to reading. Time after time, older siblings related that they utilized this technique. It's not clear where they learned this method. We can only assume it was learned in school, from a parent, or perhaps, from an older sibling of their own. One thing is certain, however—"sounding it out" was very much a part of the word attack strategy taught to beginning readers by their older siblings.

Eight-year-old Brian chose to model the process for 6-year-old Nicki:

When I read with my sister I help her with words that she doesn't know and that. I sound them out for her. I'd just start saying "men..." She starts getting it, once I start sounding it out for her.

Eight-year-old Greg also used "sounding it out" to help his 6-year-old sister through her favorite book, *Pinocchio*:

My sister can just read a little bit, so I help her. She really doesn't know Pinocchio, so I say, um, tell the parts that say "pi" and then "no," and she says "no," "keyo," and she says "key." And she said it. She says the whole word. Sometimes she forgets the word after I show her, so I show it to her again.

Natalie, age 9, used her fingers to cover and uncover parts of words to be sounded out by her 6-year-old brother, Jacob. She remarked:

I usually help him with the words because he hardly don't know a lot of them. I usually tell him to sound out. I cover part of the word like a

letter. Then he sounds out. Then he gets the word. I keep moving my
finger along the word so he can sound it out.

Jackie used a slightly different approach with her younger sister. "I make her sound it out, and then I tell her, if she doesn't know it. I usually add the first part of the word and then she usually figures the second part."

Indeed, many of the older siblings readily supplied words for the younger children when they did not know a word. Several of them seemed to supply the word whenever the younger child stumbled, miscued, or simply produced nothing. Perhaps Mike, age 9, summed it up best when he remarked:

Sometimes you just got to tell them the word. I mean they can't sound it
out, and they can't remember it, so you just tell him. Sometimes you
can't sound it out so I tell him it then. It's good to tell him the word 'cuz
it keeps him going and he doesn't lose track of what he's saying.
Sometimes if he tries to sound it out, he forgets what he was reading
and can't figure out any more words. He reads better if I tell him the
word.

Mike's comment indicated a concern for his younger brother's pacing, rhythm, and overall utilization of language knowledge as a tool for unlocking unknown or partially known words. By supplying unknown words, he was keeping the decoding process moving forward and focusing his younger brother's attention on meaning. It was clear that most sibling tutors readily supplied unknown words when teaching younger children to read. If we are to learn from these teaching experts, we should be using a combination of "sound it out" and supplying the unknown word whenever necessary to keep the language flow moving forward. Many teachers already do this and make decisions wisely as to when to employ each method. It can't hurt to be reminded, however, not to focus on one single method too much, losing sight of what an individual reader needs. More than this, the older siblings serve as a reminder to keep instruction pressure-free, nonthreatening, supportive, nurturing, and in natural settings whenever possible.

In general, it appeared that the older brother and sister "experts" employed many of the tried and true methods utilized in classrooms today. It's important to note, however, that almost all of the instruction described here occurred when the younger siblings were actually reading or being read to in trade books. Books were selected with care, especially with regard to readability level and interest. It should also be noted that very few of the older siblings interviewed mentioned paper-and-pencil tasks, workbooks, dittos, or similar commonly accepted instructional practices. It appears that these little experts, for the most part, restricted their instructional efforts to trade-type reading books. Perhaps there is also a lesson to be learned here.

A Classroom Teacher Responds...

It is refreshing to listen to children describe reading as a warm, comfortable experience. The bedtime story setting, as children describe it, appears to be an ideal learning situation because it is natural, relaxing, and free from pressure. If children are finding success in learning to read at home in this type of atmosphere, maybe I should consider a heavier dose of nonthreatening, natural reading experiences in my own classroom. The part of my day that is closest to the bedtime story experience is our afternoon storytime, when I read aloud to the children for pure pleasure. Now that I think about it, this part of our day is not only my childrens' favorite time, but my own. This is when they are totally engrossed, laugh and cry with me, and beg for more. This is when we share experiences similar to those found in the stories we read, or we discuss what it is about the story that makes it wonderful. Maybe I should listen more carefully to my students and comply more often when they beg me to read them more books. This activity may be the most important form of reading instruction I deliver all day, although the children probably will not recognize it as "instruction" at all.

I was fascinated that the children at this early age have such insight into the selection of reading materials. Having read professional books and articles on the topic of "appropriate reading material selection," I am familiar with devices such as readability formulas and interest inventories to help determine what the children should and can read. To supplement these techniques, maybe I should simply ask the children what they would like to read. A healthy balance needs to be maintained between student choice and teacher selection of reading materials. I can see the value of involving the children even more now. I suspect there will be some children who initially choose books that are too difficult or too easy, but they will tire of this practice as they realize the objective is reading for pleasure. The naturalness of the reading setting would certainly be enhanced the more children were encouraged to select their own books.

Along with a look at instructional setting and reading material selection, the children in this chapter provided an interesting glimpse into their method of reading instruction. These young teachers realize that no singular method of instruction works for all children, all the time. They understand the necessity of phonics as they instruct their younger siblings to "sound out" a word. But they also realize the importance of reading for meaning when they supply the unknown word as a child experiences reading difficulty. My favorite response was from Mike: "I mean they can't sound it out and they can't remember it, so you just tell him . . . it keeps him going and he doesn't lose track of what he's saying." I need to remember Mike's words the next time I'm scrambling for a strategy that works. The other thing that I want to keep in mind as I plan for reading instruction is the material used by the children. Children who perceived that meaningful reading instruction occurred at home by older siblings received instruction with trade books. Instruction occurred while the child was being read to and while he or she was actually reading a book. The children don't talk about worksheets or workbooks as meaningful instructional activities. Again, I don't believe that we should never ask a child to practice a skill or complete a written activity, but I do believe we need to spend more time actually reading to children, listening to them read, and conferencing as members of the same "literature club."

Such commonsense plans for reading instruction provide a natural, warm setting, involve students in selection of materials, use methods of instruction that are flexible, ensure success, and use a wide variety of high-quality books. It's not a bad plan, not a bad plan at all—and to think, the plan came from children!

Parents Respond...

In our family, older siblings definitely have played an important role in helping the younger children learn to read. Our children often read trade books to each other during the day and at bedtime. When the younger children were preschoolers and kindergartners, their older sibling(s) read to them. Late in the kindergarten year and increasingly during first grade, the younger children read to their older sibling(s), as well. Additionally, the older children have helped the younger ones with particular aspects of the learning-to-read process. Our second oldest child credited her older sister with teaching her the vowels and how to pronounce them. The oldest independently concurred that she had taught her sister "her vowels."

Our children periodically play school for hours and hours at home on weekend days. They set up elaborate classrooms in a bedroom or in the basement playroom. Makeshift desks appear. Chairs are positioned for reading group. Worksheets are taped to the walls. Storybooks are stashed in the "reading corner." Our oldest child always is the teacher because, as the younger children tell us, "She knows more . . . She's the best teacher." She leads pretend classes, complete with assignments and grades.

It makes sense that children are influenced by their siblings in learning to read. They look up to their older brothers and sisters, seek their approval, and emulate them. As they see their older siblings reading and thereby looking more and more like grown-ups, they yearn to participate, too. The older children are proud to show their skills and share their secrets for success with the younger ones.

Siblings are not the only young people who influence a child's reading development. Friends and classmates play a role. Our children tell us that their classmates are integral to the learning-to-read process at school. The more advanced readers help the slower ones. Children for whom English is a second language form a "buddy" system whereby the children who are more facile in English act as interpreters for and guide the others until those children can hold their own in the classroom. At home, when our children play school, friends frequently are included as "students" or "teachers' aides." More informally, when children have friends over they often just read to each other.

We have observed that children can be well on their way to becoming accomplished readers before entering the first grade. There appear to be a number of reasons. Sometimes older siblings have acted as teachers. Often parents have spent extensive time reading with their children. Perhaps television has provided a boost. Frequently early reading experiences in preschool and kindergarten are contributors.

We found it very interesting that, when asked who taught them to read, our two younger children both indicated that their kindergarten teachers had. They acknowledged, however, that their older sister had helped, too. Our oldest child said that her remedial reading teacher had been the one who taught her to read.

The fact that children enter the first grade with a variety of reading skills must present real challenges to the classroom teacher. Initially, assessing each child's capabilities and needs must be difficult enough. But, subsequently, to guide each child's progress given the disparities encountered must be the ultimate challenge. We would surmise, however, that it is just these demands that attract teachers to their profession in the first place.

▶ 10

Reading: Through the Child's Eyes

al attempt to explain and convince you of the importance of
looking ⎯⎯⎯⎯ d of teaching and learning through the eyes of the child. If you have not yet sat opposite a child and asked, "What is reading?," then you have missed an opportunity to embrace and understand the teachings of this book. Before you complete the last chapter, you may wish to take a few minutes to sit with a child and listen.

LISTEN TO CHILDREN

Mrs. Taylor sat down on the reading rug next to Shelly. For the past three to four months Shelly had been struggling in reading, and Mrs. Taylor was at a loss as to why. Shelly's oral reading had become slow and laborious, and she seemed to have lost the word attack skills that she formerly possessed. The school's reading specialist had tested her and prescribed phonics drills. The school psychologist reported an above-average IQ with auditory processing difficulties. The psychologist recommended a whole-word approach to reading. After three weeks of following the specialists' advice, Mrs. Taylor knew that Shelly was becoming more and more confused. Out of frustration, she pulled her chair next to Shelly's and gently asked, "What happens when you read?"

"I look at the pictures and try to remember the story," Shelly replied.

"Oh?" Mrs. Taylor paused and waited for Shelly to continue.

"You know, like you look at the picture, and it tells you what the words are going to be," Shelly explained.

"What do you do when there aren't any pictures on the page?" asked Mrs. Taylor.

"I wait for the words to come back," said Shelly.

"What does it mean to wait for the words?" Mrs. Taylor probed.

"Well, when I look at the words and think about the sounds, the letters sometimes change, and I can't sound it out anymore. You know. Sometimes I start to sound out the beginning of the word, and then I kinda lose my place. I think my eyes get a little mixed up."

"What happens then, Shelly?" asked Mrs. Taylor.

"I wait for the word to come back, but usually I lose my turn."

Mrs. Taylor didn't need to hear another word. Shelly's description of what happens when she reads had all the earmarks of a classic visual problem. She would refer Shelly immediately to a qualified vision specialist.

Two weeks later, Shelly was once again processing print with little hesitation and applying many of the decoding skills she had been taught. The vision specialist had been able to pinpoint a problem with near-point vision and had prescribed corrective lenses, which helped Shelly immediately.

Mrs. Taylor's only regret was that she waited so long to ask Shelly the question, "What happens when you read?" In six minutes Shelly was able to provide Mrs. Taylor with the information necessary to take the appropriate next step in diagnosing the problem.

Fortunately for Shelly, Mrs. Taylor had long ago learned the value of listening to children and giving credence to their perceptions. She knew that remarks like "I wait for a word to come back" did not mean that Shelly was confused, but, rather, when viewed from the child's perspective, could shed light on the problem.

Not all teachers share Mrs. Taylor's understanding of children. Many teachers would have let the opinion of the "experts" prevail and would never have thought to consult with Shelly. Still others would have dismissed Shelly's comments as being irrelevant to the problem. It is easy for adults to impose their views and interpretations of what is real, meaningful, and relevant onto children. After all, my first response to Amy Anderson's comment, "I used to think reading was making sense of a story, but now I know it is just letters" was that Amy was confused and mistaken. It was only after careful consideration and additional conversations with Amy that I came to understand the accuracy and insightfulness of her remark.

As educators, we must come to a point where our initial reaction to a child's point of view is one of acceptance. We may not immediately understand the meaning of the child's statement, but we must accept and respect it, nonetheless. Once we have accepted and recognized the statement's legitimacy, we then can begin to look for what the child actually meant. The search is often not easy and can be frustrating at times.

Initially, we should attempt to context what we have heard in child terms— that is, to take the child's remark and examine it from every conceivable angle. Amy's comment made total sense once I considered the instruction she received in class. Reading for her at this point consisted of an almost endless stream of letter sounds and letter names because that is what her reading instruction consisted of.

Additionally, we should seek further information from the child which might shed light on the concern. I learned from Amy that prior to first grade, reading had been stories. That is, she read storybooks with her parents on a regular basis, and the kindergarten experience was also heavily laden with reading stories.

This information enabled me to put Amy's remarks in an appropriate context and make sense of what she was saying. The information also had implications for instruction. That is, once Amy's teacher found out about her "definition," she was not comfortable with how Amy was currently thinking about reading. Amy's narrow view of reading was inconsistent with the goals of the reading program and the teacher. Steps were taken to expand Amy's reading experiences in school to focus more on reading for meaning.

In the case of both Amy and Shelly, we see how a child's perception can be utilized as an important teaching tool. Children's perceptions clearly should be viewed as an important component of sound instructional decision making.

The research findings reported in the preceding chapters of this book will enable us to understand first-graders' perceptions of reading. The inquiry process described, listening questions in particular, should serve as a model for teachers in their pursuit of a better understanding of reading through the eyes of the learner.

My research findings are consistent with a perspective advanced by Harste, Woodward, and Burke (1984), which recognizes children like Amy as competent, active, accomplished learners. The authors contend, "Researchers studying what young children know about print have found children in a state of 'cognitive confusion.' After many years of work in this area, however, we have yet to find a child who is 'cognitively confused'" (p. 15). They give numerous concrete examples showing children's rich understandings. Based on a study of kindergartners (Woodward, 1977) and observations of preschool and first-grade classrooms (Harste & Burke, 1977), Harste et al. explain:

> We began this program of research assuming that what the young children knew about reading and writing prior to first grade far exceeded what teachers and beginning reading and writing programs assumed. Now after six years of research and involvement in a wide variety of analysis, we realize we were not optimistic enough. Children know much more than any of us have ever dared to imagine. (p. 77)

Children enter school knowing a great deal about reading and writing, and they are able to demonstrate and articulate that understanding. My research also supports those who advance the position that young children engage in many critical literacy behaviors long before they participate in conventional instruction. The concept of emergent literacy (Clay, 1979; Holdaway, 1979; Teale & Sulzby, 1986) has been suggested as a way of characterizing this understanding of early literacy development. This perspective of emergent literacy has in fact helped to legitimize beginning readers' perceptions and provide the springboard for serious investigation of how children think about reading and how these perceptions come to be.

It is critical for educators to understand the world of reading through a child's eyes. Research in the sociology and psychology of literacy learning over the past ten years (Cochran-Smith, 1984; Goodman, 1985; Graves, 1983; Harste, Woodward, & Burke, 1984; Jaggar and Smith-Burke, 1985; Taylor, 1983; Templeton, 1986) has illustrated that learning is a cooperative, negotiated process in which the perceptions and motivation of the students are crucial. Researchers argue for ways of reconceptualizing literacy learning that account for the variety and sophistication of children's perspectives. Seeing children as active interpreters of the reading environment calls for teachers to examine carefully the effects of their own behaviors on their students.

CHILDREN HAVE RICH PERCEPTIONS

The findings of my research with first-graders clearly indicate that they have rich perceptions of reading that are influenced significantly by their surroundings. What goes on in reading groups, in class, and at home determines children's perceptions of what reading is. Comments such as "Reading is stand up sit down" or "Reading is when we take our pencils and come up front" suggest that first-graders' perceptions take on a physical activity component. Remarks like, "In reading we put X's in the boxes" and "We do worksheets" indicate that children's perceptions are formed by the paper-and-pencil tasks utilized by teachers in the instructional process.

Beginning readers also know how well they are doing and have feelings about their progress in school. They chart their own progress in reading by analyzing instructional materials. They understand that books containing pages with no pictures and numerous sentences on a page are "harder" than books with pages that contain only one or two words in isolation. "Neutral" group designations by teachers, such as Red, Blue, and Green or Yankees, Dodgers, and Pirates, do not seem to interfere with first-graders' ability to understand which groups are high, medium, and low. Hard- and soft-cover books are a real tip-off to first-graders and, in and of themselves, take on a great deal of significance. Being in a hard-cover book is a symbol to be worn proudly. As Douglas remarked, "Did you notice I'm in a hard-cover book?" First-graders can feel "good," "sad," "happy," "glad," or even "confused" when they read. Some "don't like to think about it" while others want to read "more and more" or "all the time." First-graders have also developed many purposes for reading. Some read for informational or environmental purposes and others for recreational or instructional purposes.

It is important that teachers and researchers alike remember that first-graders are able to "track" progress and to recognize the impact of their progress on their feelings about themselves as readers. It is also important to remember that perceptions are colored by reading both at home and at school. Take, for instance, the remarks Danny shared with me one day as we talked about reading:

> *I was in Mrs. T's class for kindergarten. Then I moved up to Mrs. J's class for first grade. Then I came to first grade again because my reading group was too low. I wasn't in the higher group yet. Now I'm in a little higher group. Reading is reading book and workbook. I only like to read at reading group. I don't like to read alone because I can't read*

most of the words. They're a little too big and a little too long. I try to sound them out but can't. I like it when my Mom reads to me and my sister. Thinking about reading makes me feel uncomfortable. I'm not good at it. I like to think about my farm. I know everything about that.

This continuous quotation depicts how Danny thinks about reading and shows the various elements present in children's perceptions. The structure of this quotation was uninterrupted by any comments or prompts.

We must also recognize that factors such as positive and negative feedback, structure and control, and home and school environments are all inextricably intertwined, and that they have a significant impact on how children view reading. Consider the following snapshot of an actual first-grade classroom.

Teacher: I'd like to see my "Green" group. Please remember when we come up we tiptoe so that we do not disturb these wonderful workers at their seats. (The group begins to review the master words from last year.)

Maxine: (Pointing at the word *look*) This word is *see* (The teacher shakes her head no.) Oh, it's *look*, but both of these words [*look* and *see*] mean the same thing.

Teacher: They do mean the same thing, but how do you know *look* is not *see*? What does *look* start with? (Teacher holds up a list of words.) Do you know any of these words, Maxine? (Maxine shakes her head no.)

Teacher: You'll learn them fast because you are a smart little girl. You had different words in your school. Now you'll have to learn our words. (They begin to play a word recognition game, and each child gets to demonstrate knowledge of words.)

Teacher: Paula, you got all of the words correct, so you get your hand stamped. Excellent!

Teacher: Mike, I'm sorry, you missed the word *the*, and you must read all of the words correctly in order to get a stamp. I can't give you a stamp because you missed a word, but I am so proud of you, especially since you were not in this school last year and don't know "our" words yet.

Mike: My mom says I'm a fast learner.

Teacher: You are! There is proof of it right here. You only missed one word, and you didn't even go to this school last year.

Teacher: Debbie, will you read the list of words? (To the rest of the group) Debbie only knew one word at the beginning of first grade. Let's see how many she knows now. (Debbie reads the entire list correctly.)

Teacher: Be sure you tell your mommy that. Another fast learner! Debbie, let me stamp your hand.

Teacher: You may go quietly back to your seats.

This scenario of one first-grade classroom illustrates how children can (and usually do) receive both positive and negative feedback from teachers, and how children seem to connect that feedback to parental feedback. "My mom says I'm a fast learner." It also illustrates how teachers forge a link in the home–school perception loop by encouraging children to "Be sure you tell your mommy that." When one observes and reflects upon the feedback loops that exist in classrooms and in homes of first-graders, it is not surprising that first-graders develop real and deep feelings about themselves as readers and about reading in general.

I have come to understand that first-graders' perceptions don't always mesh with the perceptions held by the adult world. Consider for instance, the first-grader who, when asked what reading was, said, "Reading is music." When the youngster was asked to explain what she meant, she said:

When I started piano lessons I could not read the notes. When I came to reading, I could not read the words. My friend, she takes piano, too; she taught me to just make up the music that I couldn't play. That's what I used to do when I couldn't really read my books, just make up the story as I went along. Now I can read G clef and all the notes and play a song. I learned to read books the same way. Practice.

The way in which this student viewed reading is an example of a perception of reading that differs greatly from reading perceptions held by adults. Most adults would agree that reading is not music. We now know, however, that the child's perception of reading, or what reading has come to mean to her, has useful implications for teachers and is extremely important as we consider how reading is acquired. Wouldn't it have been useful for a teacher to have used the piano–reading analogy with this child as an assist in teaching her how to unlock unknown words through the use of context?

Indeed, children's perceptions may often be inconsistent with the goals stated by adults or the objectives, of reading programs. They are, however, real, valid, and rich perceptions and should not be dismissed as being confused, immature, or inferior. This is the essence of my research and of this book.

Children have a logic of their own, and they often think in ways that are qualitatively different from those of adults. For example, in a study analyzing children's responses to Dr. Seuss's *The Butter Battle Book* (an allegory in which the imaginary Zooks and Yooks fight over which side of bread should be buttered), a number of children described the theme as "Never butter bread with the butter side down." Most adults would agree that Dr. Seuss depicted the two sides in this story as fighting over something trivial, something that really doesn't matter, so that their fighting and building weapons against each other was absurd. Therefore, it would be easy to conclude that the children who thought that one side was buttering their bread "the right way" and the other side was buttering their bread "the wrong way" were confused and did not understand the point of the story. However, the researchers pointed out that one child went on to explain in his response that if he buttered his bread on the down side, he would get butter on his pants and his mother would get mad. He completed his response with a picture of a hand dropping pants into a washing machine. Once the situation is understood from the child's perspective, the conclusion can be reached that the adults who think it doesn't matter which side bread is buttered on are the ones who are wrong! So, whenever children's answers seem confused or wrong to us, it's a good idea to probe for more information and to listen respectfully to their explanations (Kane and Gentile, 1987).

From the beginning, this study was designed with the intention of looking at reading from the perspective of the child. Fortunately, early in the process, a freckle-faced 6-year-old, the aforementioned Amy, when asked, "What is reading?," turned her head, thought a bit, and said, "I used to think reading was making sense of a story, but now I know it is just letters."

Years of reading research and practice, and it takes a 6-year-old child's simple, succinct statement to say it all. This somewhat disturbing response reminds us that we must listen to children and accept their perspective. It also suggests that children bring a rich understanding to reading, and that this understanding is meaning-oriented and is learned at home. We must also recognize that this perception is altered as a result of the educational process, and, more often than not, first-graders' perceptions shift from focusing on meaning to concentrating on instructional tasks.

Future reading research and practice must not assume that truth begins and ends with adult definitions. A great deal of research and subsequent instruction has occurred on the basis of what researchers and teachers think children know about reading. Examination of work that children produce, categorization of superficial responses to interview questions, and standardized tests are all ways in which researchers and educators determine what children know about reading. From data gathered in this manner, we make inferences and draw conclusions about what and how children learn. If researchers and educators want to learn what children know and how they perceive reading, they must acquire this knowledge just as they would from a respected colleague or friend who has valuable information. We must ask children questions and spend time with them until we understand the child's perspective.

GAUGING INSTRUCTIONAL EFFECTIVENESS

If we accept the premise that children have rich and valid understandings of reading, then we can utilize children's perceptions as one gauge of instructional effectiveness. Children's perceptions should be monitored on a regular basis.

Categories of perceptions have been created through children's articulations of what reading means to them and can serve as a framework for helping teachers ascertain their own important information regarding the perceptions of children in their classrooms. These categories are examined in earlier chapters of this book:

1. What they do in reading (tasks)
2. How they learn to read (process)
3. Purposes for reading
4. How well they are doing
5. How they feel about reading
6. Standardized testing
7. Reading at home and reading at school
8. Siblings as teachers.

By better understanding how children perceive reading and themselves as readers, teachers can better facilitate continuing growth and build upon what children already know. Such information can also help teachers understand if the child's perception of reading is consistent with the teacher's and can provide a sound theoretical base for classroom practice. We must also include the child's perspective and acknowledge its power to advance and enrich future early literacy acquisition research and practice.

Finally, it is my greatest hope that this book may further develop our sensitivity to children and their world and instill in us respect and appreciation for their insights and abilities. If I could envision the "perfect" classroom, it would have Amy, Danny, Mary, and other children providing valuable direction and insight to teachers who listen more than they talk. It would have parents of first-graders reading books to their children at home without the frustration of completing unfinished work or lists of words to memorize. Most important, it would have children who are comfortable learning to read in a way that makes sense to them. We must listen to children to make this happen, include the child's perspective, and acknowledge its power to advance and enrich early literacy acquisition. Children have much to tell us.

A Classroom Teacher Responds...

"Through the eyes of children"... These words take on new meaning as I finish reading this book. My eyes have been opened a little wider, and my heart has been touched a bit deeper, as I strive to better understand the children I teach. The message is clear. If I channel my energies toward more "kidwatching, kid listening, and kid understanding," I may develop better methods for reading instruction and produce a healthier climate to promote the love of reading.

How difficult is it to get an honest, accurate answer from a child? How much and how often do I need to delve into the child's world to ascertain how they feel and what they need? I was fascinated by many of the children's responses to reading in this study. I wondered if the children I teach would answer in similar ways. I needed to find out, so I took the author's challenge to become teacher-researcher and conducted my own mini-study, with one first-grader and his third-grade sibling. Would these two children provide insight into the reading process as did those children interviewed by Dr. Michel?

My first attempt was direct and discouraging. "What is reading?" I asked 6-year-old Jon. "It is boring," he replied. "I like math." This idea of talking to children to gain a wealth of knowledge did not appear to be working. I tried a few more questions about reading, but this youngster would only discuss the thrill of mathematics. I gave up and continued my daily lessons. A few days later, Jon was quietly reading a storybook, so I gathered up my courage and tried again. I remembered reading earlier in this book that direct questioning of the student may seem artificial and not make children feel comfortable enough to share what they know. I decided to involve Jon in a more natural dialogue. I started talking to him about the story he was reading, and he eagerly responded. In the midst of this conversation, I asked, "What is reading?"

Jon immediately said, "Reading…it is kind of fun. You can learn a lot. It tells me things I don't know about. It can teach me things."

I was on a roll, so I continued, "How did you learn to read?"

Jon responded, "My teacher shows me words and says them for about a month. I get used to them and then I can sound them out."

I then asked Jon, "Do you sound out every word?"

"No, some words I just read. I say them. I don't need to sound out words that I already know!" replied Jon disgustedly to my ignorant question.

I decided to ask Jon to share with me who actually was responsible for teaching him to read. He quickly responded, "Can I answer more than one?," indicating that he still thought there were rules to be followed during this interchange. I explained to him that there were no right and wrong answers, and that I truly wanted to know what he had to say. He seemed to like that. Jon very slowly explained, "My Mom—she showed what reading is and read me stories. My teacher—she taught me a lot. She went over words. I read books with her, and other books by myself. My sister—she reads books to me." This is incredible, I thought. Did he read this book? I had to find out more, so I continued. When I asked what he liked best about reading, he replied, "You get to learn stuff." When I asked him the worst part about reading, he emphatically said, "Anybody knows that! It takes too long and sometimes it's pretty boring. It's not really that boring to me but some kids hate it. They don't like reading. The chapters can be boring. My book has lots of chapters. It will probably take me the rest of the year." It became clear through our discussion that Jon was referring to his preprimer, as he explained that each of the stories was like a new chapter. When discussing his school reading books further, he commented, "These are O.K., but I'd rather read my own books. I like to choose them."

I realized that it was time for Jon to go to lunch, so I asked one last question: "What advice would you give to a kindergarten child who wants to learn to read?"

Jon seriously remarked, "Read a lot. Ask your parents to make a list of words and read them to you. You will remember them, and you will soon be able to read chapter books."

It was true. Jon did have a lot to say. He provided insights regarding methods of learning and reading preferences that I would never have guessed. I now know that Jon prefers choosing his own reading materials. He also shared that his method of word attack is based predominately on the whole word, as he describes looking at a word, listening to that word, and saying that word.

I wanted to continue my mini-study, so I met with one of Jon's "reading teachers"...his 8-year-old sister, Katie. By this point, I felt more comfortable with the interview process and confidently said, "Jon tells me that you helped in teaching him to read. How did you do that?"

She replied quite positively, "I challenge him. I give him a big list of books to read and have him check off every book he finishes. If a book is too hard I tell him to skip it. He should not have to read a book that is too hard. I try to choose books that he will like and that are easy enough for him."

I then asked Katie, "What if a book is easy, but he doesn't know a certain word? What do you tell him?"

Katie answered, "He should read the rest of the sentence and then go back to the word he doesn't know. He will figure it out. That's what works for my brother."

What a wonderful strategy! I may invite Katie to our next faculty workshop to discuss meaningful methods of reading instruction. My mini-study convinced me that the theme woven throughout this book, "Listen to children," is a simple message but a powerful tool. Children do have a rich understanding of reading. By listening to children and understanding their perspectives, I truly have the ability to enhance, rather than extinguish, my students' early literacy learnings.

Parents Respond...

In simplest terms, this book is about one thing—communication. The author argues persuasively that for children to develop most effectively as readers, there must be frequent, meaningful communication among teacher, parent, and child. Each of these participants in the communication process—teacher, parent, child—has something important to contribute and should be heard. The teacher is the natural focal point for stimulating and shaping this communication. The teacher can sift through the information gleaned from the ongoing communication process to piece together plans early in the school year for dealing with individual students and subsequently to adjust those plans throughout the year.

Our school administration tells us that the best thing we can do to help our children in school is become involved in the schools. In effect, we are being drawn into the communication process. We are encouraged to get involved by volunteering to chaperone field trips; by participating in open house; by talking with teachers whenever something is on our mind; and/or by coming to watch our children take part in school concerts, plays, and programs. After reading this book, we've talked about volunteering in our children's classrooms, perhaps as readers or listeners. We find that our children are proud to see us involved. They communicate better with us when they know that we care and that we can relate to what they're doing in school.

Discussions with our children as we have pondered this book and tested its findings have given us wonderful new insights on our children's views on reading, on learning in general, and about our relationships with our children and their teachers. Listening to children in the ways advocated by this book definitely can make teachers more effective in the classroom and us better parents. Clearly this is worth doing!

It occurs to us that most of the author's observations apply not only to reading but also to other instructional areas such as writing and math. Teachers might want to reflect on how they can extend the lessons learned here to all of their classroom teaching. It should be time well spent.

Our youngest child summed it all up recently when he described his first-grade teacher, "She's a really good teacher. She's nice. She teaches us lots of stuff, and she's fun." What more could a teacher want her students to say about her?

We have changed since reading this book. We are spending more time listening to our children talk about their learning. We are amazed by the richness of their insights.

References

Allington, R. L. (1983). The reading instruction provided readers of differing reading abilities. *Elementary School Journal, 83,* 548–559.

Amarel, M. (1980). *The teacher as observer.* Harrisburg: Pennsylvania Department of Education, Right to Read office.

Atwell, N. (1987). *In the middle.* Portsmouth, NH: Boynton/Cook.

Baker, L., & Brown, A. L. (1984). Cognitive monitoring in reading. In J. Flood (Ed.), *Understanding reading comprehension* (pp. 21–44). Newark, DE: International Reading Association.

Becker, H. (1970). Field work evidence. *Sociological work.* Chicago: Aldine.

Becker, H. S., Geer, B., Hughes, E. C., & Strauss, A. (1961). *Boys in white: Student culture in medical school.* Chicago: University of Chicago Press.

Blumer, H. (1969). *Symbolic interaction: Perspective and method.* Englewood Cliffs, NJ: Prentice-Hall.

Bogdan, R. (1972). *Participant observation in organizational settings.* Syracuse, NY: Syracuse University Press.

Bogdan, R. (1982). *Illiterate or learning disabled?: A symbolic interactionist approach to the social dimensions of reading and writing.* Presented at the International Reading Association, Syracuse, New York.

Bogdan, R., & Biklen, S. (1982). *Qualitative research for education: An introduction to theory and methods.* Boston: Allyn and Bacon.

Boljonis, A., & Hinchman, K. (1987). *First graders' perceptions of reading and writing.* Paper presented at the annual meeting of the National Reading Conference, St. Petersburg, Florida.

Bondy, E. (1985). *Children's definitions of reading: Products of an interactive process.* Paper presented at the Annual Meeting of the American Educational Research Association, Chicago.

Butler, D. (1979). *Cushla and her books.* Boston: The Horn Book.

Calkins, L. M. (1983). *Lessons from a child.* Exeter, NH: Heinemann Educational Books.

Calkins, L. M. (1986). *The art of teaching writing.* Exeter, NH: Heinemann Educational Books.

Clay, M. M. (1979). *Reading: The patterning of complex behavior.* Portsmouth, NH: Heinemann.

Cochran-Smith, M. (1984). *The making of a reader.* Norwood, NJ: Ablex.

Dahlgren, G., & Olsson, L. (1986). *The child's conception of reading.* Paper presented at the Seventieth Annual Meeting of the American Educational Research Association, San Francisco. (ERIC Document Reproduction Service No. ED 268 497)

Denny, T., & Weintraub, S. (1963). Exploring first-graders' concepts of reading. *The Reading Teacher, 16,* 363–365.

Denny, T. P., & Weintraub, S. (1966). First graders' responses to three questions about reading. *Elementary School Journal, 66,* 441–448.

Downing, J. (1969). How children think about reading. *The Reading Teacher, 23,* 217–230.

Downing, J. (1970). Children's concepts of language in learning to read. *Educational Research, 12,* 101–112.

Durkin, D. (1966). *Children who read early.* New York: Teachers College Press.

Francis, H. (1973). Children's experience of reading and notions of units in language. *British Journal of Educational Psychology, 43,* 17–23.

Glaser, B. G., & Strauss, A. L. (1967). *The discovery of grounded theory: Strategies for qualitative research.* Chicago: Aldine.

Goodman, Y. (1977). Kidwatching: An alternative to testing. *Elementary Principal, 57,* 41–45.

Goodman, Y. (1985). Kidwatching: observing children in the classroom. In A. Jaggar & M. T. Smith-Burke (Eds.), *Observing the language learner* (pp. 9–18). Newark, DE: International Reading Association.

Graves, D. (1983). *Writing: Teachers and children at work.* Portsmouth, NH: Heinemann Educational Books.

Harste, J. C., & Burke, C. L. (1977). A new hypothesis for reading teacher research: Both teaching and learning of reading are theoretically based. In P. D. Pearson (Ed.), *Reading: Research, theory and practice* (Twenty-sixth yearbook of the National Reading Conference) (pp. 32–40). Minneapolis, MN: Mason.

Harste, J. C., Burke, C. L., & Woodward, V.A. (1981). Children's language and world: Initial encounters with print. In J. Langer & M. Smith-Burke (Eds.), *Reader meets author: Bridging the gap* (pp. 105–131). Newark, DE: International Reading Association.

Harste, J., Woodward, V., & Burke, C. (1984). *Language stories and literacy lessons.* Portsmouth, NH: Heinemann Educational Books.

Hiebert, E. H. (1983). An examination of ability grouping for reading instruction. *Reading Research Quarterly, 18,* 231–255.

Holdaway, D. (1979). *The foundations of literacy.* Portsmouth, NH: Heinemann Educational Books.

Holt, J. (1989). *Learning all the time.* Reading, MA: Addison-Wesley.

Huey, E. B. (1908). *The psychology and pedagogy of reading.* Cambridge, MA: MIT Press.

Jaggar, A., & Smith-Burke, M. T. (Eds.). (1985). *Observing the language learner.* Newark, DE: International Reading Association.

Johns, J. (1972). Children's concepts of reading and their reading achievement. *Journal of Reading Behavior, 4,* 56–57.

Johns, J. (1974). Concepts of reading among good and poor readers. *Education, 95,* 58–60.

Johns, J. (1986). Student's perceptions of reading: Thirty years of inquiry. In D. Yaden & S. Templeton (Eds.), *Metalinquistic awareness and beginning literacy* (pp. 31–40). Portsmouth, NH: Heinemann Educational Books.

Johns, J., & Ellis, D. (1976). Reading: Children tell it like it is. *Reading World, 16* (2), 115–128.

Johnston, P. H. (1992). *Constructive evaluation of literate activity.* White Plains, NY: Longman.

Kane, S., & Gentile, C. (1987). *Diverse responses to literature: Issues teachers face.* Presented at the National Reading Conference, St. Petersburg, Florida.

Lindfors, J. W. (1984). How children learn or how teachers teach? A profound confusion. *Language Arts, 61*(6), 600–606.

Long, R., Manning, G., & Manning, M. (1985). *High and low achieving first-grade readers' perceptions of the reading process.* Paper presented at the Fourteenth Annual Meeting of the Mid-South Educational Research Association, Biloxi, Mississippi. (ERIC Document Reproduction Service No. ED 266 429)

Mason, J. M. (1967). Preschoolers' concepts of reading. *The Reading Teacher, 21,* 130–132.

Mayfield, M. I. (1983). Code systems instruction and kindergarten children's perceptions of the nature and purpose of reading. *Journal of Educational Research, 76,* 161-168.

Michel, P., (1990). What first graders think about reading. In R. W. Blake (Ed.), *Whole language explorations and applications* (pp. 41–46). Schenectady: New York State English Council.

Oliver, M. E. (1975). The development of language concepts of preprimary Indian children. *Language Arts, 52,* 865–869.

Pearson, P. D., & Johnson, D. D. (1978). *Teaching reading comprehension.* New York: Holt, Rinehart & Winston.

Pikulski, J. J. (1989). The assessment of reading: A time for change? *The Reading Teacher, 43* (1), 80–81.

Reardon, S. J. (1990). Putting reading tests in their place. *The New Advocate, 1* (1), 29–37.

Reid, J. F. (1966), Learning to think about reading. *Educational Research, 9,* 56–62.

Routman, R. (1988). *Transitions from literature to literacy.* Portsmouth, NH: Heinemann Educational Books.

Shannon, P. (1989). *Broken promises: Reading instruction in twentieth-century America.* Granby, MA: Bergin and Garvey.

Smith, F. (1983). *Essays into literacy.* Portsmouth, NH: Heinemann Educational Books.

Smith, F. (1990). *To think.* New York: Teachers College Press.

Swanson, B. B. (1985). Listening to students about reading. *Reading Horizons, 22,* 123–128.

Taylor, D. (1983). *Family literacy.* Exeter, NH: Heinemann Educational Books.

Taylor, D. (1990). Teaching without testing: Assessing the complexity of children's literacy learning. *English Education, 22* (1), 4–75.

Teale, W. H. (1978). Positive environments for learning to read: What studies of early readers tell us. *Language Arts, 55,* 922–932.

Teale, W. (1984). Reading to young children: Its significance for literacy development. In H. Goelman, A. Oberg, & F. Smith, (Eds.), *Awakening to literacy* (pp. 110–121). Exeter, NH: Heinemann Educational Books.

Teale, W., & Sulzby, E. (1986). Emergent literacy as a perspective for examining how young children become writers and readers. In W. Teale & E. Sulzby (Eds.), *Emergent literacy: Writing and reading* (pp. vii–xxv). Norwood, NJ: Ablex.

Templeton, S. (1986). Literacy, readiness and basals. *The Reading Teacher, 39,* 66–82.

Trelease, J. (1990). *The new read aloud handbook.* New York: Penguin Books.

Vernon, M. D. (1957). *Backwardness in reading: A study of its nature and origin.* London: Cambridge University Press.

Weintraub, S., & Denny, T. P. (1965). What do beginning first graders say about reading? *Childhood Education, 41,* 326–327.

Weiss, J., & Hagen, R. (1988). A key to literacy: Kindergartners' awareness of the functions of print. *The Reading Teacher, 41* (6) 574–578.

Winne, P. H., & Marx, R. W. (1982). Students' and teachers' views of thinking processes involved in classroom learning. *Elementary School Journal, 82,* 493–518.

Woodward, V. A. (1977). *Comparison of early readers and non-readers in strategies of organization in intellectual tasks.* Sabbatical Leave Research Report, Indiana University, Bloomington.

Yaden, D. (1984). Reading research in metalinguistic awareness: Findings, problems, and classroom applications. *Visible Language, 18* (1), 5–47.

►

Works
Mentioned

Berry, C. E. (Ed.). (1988). *Wheels and wings.* Virginia: Time-Life Books.

Bridwell, Norman. (1988). *Clifford wants a cookie.* New York: Scholastic.

Brown, Margaret Wise. (1975/1947). *Goodnight moon.* New York: Harper & Row.

Burton, Virginia. (1939). *Mike Mulligan and his steam shovel.* Boston: Houghton Mifflin.

Cleary, Beverly. (1968). *Ramona the pest.* New York: Dell Publishing Company.

Collodi, Carlo. *Pinocchio.* (1904). (Walter S. Cramp, trans.). Boston: Ginn.

Disney, Walt. (1986). *Sleeping Beauty.* New York: Gallery Books.

Disney, Walt. (1986). *Snow White and the seven dwarfs.* New York: Gallery Books.

Galdone, Paul, (1973). *The three billy goats gruff.* Boston: Houghton Mifflin.

Hoban, Lillian. (1974). *Arthur's honey bear.* New York: Scholastic.

Kellogg, Steven. (1986). *Best friends.* New York: Trumpet Club.

Parish, Peggy. (1963). *Amelia Bedelia.* New York: Scholastic.

Rey, H. A. (1973). *Curious George.* Boston: Houghton Mifflin.

Seuss, Dr. (1960). *Green eggs and ham.* New York: Random House.

Seuss, Dr. (1984). *The butter battle book.* New York: Random House.

Sobol, D. J. (1974). *Encyclopedia Brown.* New York: Thomas Nelson.

Index

A

Ability grouping in teaching reading,
88–89. *See also* Reading.
Amelia Bedelia, 112
Arthur's Honeybear (Hoban), 52
Atwell, N., 38–39

B

Baker, L., 3
Basal reading programs, 68–69, 116
vs. independent reading, 19–20
Becker, H. S., 11, 12
Best Friends (Kellogg), 66
Biklen, S., 12, 21
Blumer, H., 12
Bogdan, R., 11, 12, 21
Boljonis, A., 87
Bondy, E., 3
Broken Promises (Shannon), 58, 116
Brown, A. L., 3
Burke, C. L., 4, 8, 9, 11, 138
Burton, V. L., 10
Butler, D., 72
Butter Battle Book, The (Dr. Seuss), 141

C

Calkins, L. M., 8
Children's self-evaluation of reading
ability, 80–85, 87–88, 91, 139

influence of negative feedback on,
85–86, 87, 140–141
influence of positive feedback on,
140–141
A Classroom Teacher Responds ...,
12–13, 29–30, 48–49, 61–62, 73–74,
89–90, 106–107, 119–120, 132–133,
143–145
Clay, M. M., 119, 138
Cleary, B., 10
Clifford Wants a Cookie, 129
Cochran-Smith, M., 138
Comprehension-oriented approach to
teaching reading, 3, 56–57. *See also*
Reading.
Criterion Referenced Reading Test
(Montgomery County Public
Schools), 103–105

D

Dahlgren, G., 8
Denny, T., 3, 6, 73
Disney, Walt, 121
Downing, J., 6, 8
Durkin, D., 117

E

Ellis, D., 7
Encyclopedia Brown, 29

F

Francis, H., 5

G

Geer, B., 11
Gentile, C., 142
Glaser, B. G., 12, 19
Goodman, Y., 4, 102, 138
Goodnight Moon, 14
Graves, D., 4, 138
Green Eggs and Ham (Dr. Seuss), 124

H

Hagen, R., 8
Harste, J. C., 4, 8, 9, 11, 138
Hinchman, K., 87
Hoban, L., 52
Holdaway, D., 138
Holt, John, 56, 117
Hom reading vs. school reading, 43–46,
    116
Homework, 112, 116
    as influence on attitudes about read-
        ing, 112, 115, 116
    parent involvement in, 113–116, 117
    as source of negative feelings, 113
Huey, E. B., 119
Hughes, E. C., 11

I

In the Middle (Atwell), 38–39
Iowa Tests of Basic Skills, 99

J

Jaggar, A., 8, 138
Johns, J., 3, 5, 7
Johnston, P. H., 102

K

Kane, S., 142
Kellogg, S., 66

L

Learning All the Time (Holt), 56, 117
Lindfors, J. W., 46
Listening questions, 23–27, 29, 30–31.
    See also Reading.
Literacy. *See also* Reading.
    definition of, 2
    emergent, 138
    in the family, 112, 117
Long, R., 8

M

Manning, G., 8
Manning, M., 8
Marx, R. W., 47
Mason, J. M., 6–7, 9
Mayfield, M. I., 3
Methodology of reading program analy-
    sis, 20–24, 26–28
Michel, P., 8
Mike Mulligan and His Steam Shovel
    (Burton), 10, 128
"Mr. Rogers' Neighborhood," 73, 121

N

Native American children, and attitudes
    about reading, 7
New Kids at the Polk Street School, The,
    112
New Read Aloud Handbook, The (Tre-
    lease), 117, 120

O

Observing the Language Learner (Jaggar
    and Smith–Burke), 8
Oliver, M. E., 3, 7, 9
Olsson, L., 8
101 Dalmatians (video), 121
Oral reading, 19
    and sounding out new words, 52–56,
        57, 58–60, 62, 130–131

P

Parents as Reading Partners (PARP), 120
Parents Respond ..., 13–15, 30–31,
  49–50, 62–63, 74–75, 90–91, 107–
  108, 120–121, 133–134, 145–146
Parent-Teacher Association, 21
Pikulski, J. J., 102
Pinocchio, 130

R

Ramona the Pest (Cleary), 10
Reading
  ability grouping in teaching of, 88–89
  children's perceptions of, 2, 3–5, 35–
    36, 37, 43–48, 56–57, 60–61, 68–69,
    71–73, 137–138, 139–140, 141–143
  classmates' influence on, 133–134
  comprehension-oriented approach to
    teaching of, 3, 56–57
  early research on teaching of, 5–7
  for enjoyment, 70–72
  home influence on, 43, 45, 111–112
  and listening questions, 23–27, 29,
    30–31
  parents' involvement in, 5, 117–119
  peer influrnces on, 90–91
  physical tasks and teaching of, 35–36,
    37–40, 42, 43, 46–48
  purposeful, 68–70
  recent studies of teaching of, 8–11,
    138
  remedial, 134
  siblings' involvement in, 125–131
  and vision problems, 136–137
  whole-word approach to learning of,
    136
  and word recognition strategy, 54
Reardon, J., 103, 105
Reid, J. F., 3, 5, 6
Remedial reading, 134. *See also* Reading.
Routman, R., 89

S

"Sesame Street," 43, 73, 121

Seuss, Dr., 124, 141
Shannon, P., 9, 58, 116
Silverstein, S., 129
Sleeping Beauty (video), 121
Smith, F., 4, 70
Smith-Burke, M. T., 8, 138
Standardized testing
  alternatives to, 102–103
  children's perceptions of, 95–96, 98–
    99
  controversy regarding, 102
  parents' role in, 99–102, 107
  practice in, 97–98, 103–105
  preparation for, 96–97, 99, 100–102,
    105
Strauss, A. L., 11, 12, 19
Sulzby, E., 138
Swanson, B. B., 8, 46
Symbolic interactionism, 12

T

Taylor, D., 102, 112, 117, 119, 126, 138
Teaching reading. *See also* Reading.
  ability grouping in, 88–89
  comprehension–oriented approach
    to, 3, 56–57
  early research on, 5–7
  and listening questions, 23–27, 29,
    30–31
  physical tasks and, 35–36, 37–40, 42,
    43, 46–48
  recent studies of, 8–11, 138
  whole-word approach to, 136
  and word recognition strategy, 54
Teale, W., 11, 117, 119, 138
Templeton, S., 11, 138
Three Billy Goats Gruff, The, 81
Time-Life, 66
Transitions from Literature to Literacy
  (Routman), 89
Trelease, J., 117, 120

V

Vernon, M. D., 6
Vision problems, and reading, 136–137.
  See also Reading.

W

Weintraub, S., 3, 6, 73
Weiss, J., 8
Wheels and Wings (Time-Life),
66
Where in the World Is Carmen Sandi-
ego?' (TV show), 63

Winne, P. H., 47
Woodward, V. A., 4, 8, 9, 11, 138
Word recognition strategy in teaching
reading, 54. *See also* Reading.

Y

Yaden, D., 7